THE

FROM.

THE VIEW FROM EDEN

TALKS TO STUDENTS OF ORGONOMY - PRACTICAL INSIGHTS INTO THE VITAL WORK OF DR. WILHELM REICH

JEROME EDEN

DEDICATION AND ACKNOWLEDGMENT

This work is dedicated to the Students of the Future and to all who strive to *Focus on Life*, on the essential in Life—that is, Love, Work and Knowledge.

It is my hope also that renewed interest will be kindled in the important work of the late Joseph Wheless, whose biblical critique *Is It God's Word?* reveals armored man's irrational conceptions of God.

FIRST EDITION

© 1976 by Jerome Eden

Printed in the United States of America

CONTENTS

INTRODUCTION

Since 1959, when I was dismissed as an educator for advocating facts and ideas contained in this book, I have been a teacher without students. Necessity forced me to express in books and articles what I was not permitted to communicate in a classroom. And while this has widened my potential audience, it has deprived me of the pleasure of contact with young people.

In one way the sequestration was beneficial, as it gave me the opportunity to publish my previous three books, *Orgone Energy, Planet in Trouble,* and *Animal Magnetism and the Life Energy,* in which I strive to focus attention on the vital work of Dr. Wilhelm Reich.

Now, in a series of "talks," I strive again to focus on The Life Energy and how it functions in man and his universe. My desire is that the student will gain some practical insight into what is important and what is unimportant in daily living, that he or she will be happier thereby, or at least understand what is obstructing happiness in human life.

"Truth" is one's immediate contact with reality. As your contact deepens, you will become more aware of the pervasive social insanity of armored man, and perhaps you will find ways to stop the insanity, the chronic murder of Christ, as Wilhelm Reich referred to it.

Our planetary populace is presently undergoing great upheavals. Where this will lead mankind cannot be known. I do know, however, that without Knowledge of Life, of

7

what *the living* is all about, "happiness and freedom" are merely empty slogans. That is why I *focus on life*. And that is why I have written this book.

JEROME EDEN
Careywood, Idaho

PLEASURE

Whatever we do voluntarily we do because it gives us pleasure or relieves anxiety. I read two items this morning in two different papers about young men: One is a 17-year-old businessman who is making $25,000 a year. Commendable. What disturbed me, however, was the young man's remark: "If there's money in it, I'll do anything. I'm lousy with girls and I'm lousy at sports, but I'm good at making money."

Making money has become a substitute for the rational pleasure of enjoying the company of girls. There is nothing wrong with making money. But money is most often a substitute for love. By the time he is 27, this young man will no doubt be a millionaire. Money can buy us things; but it cannot bring us deep or lasting pleasure as a pursuit in itself.

We have to make a distinction between rational and irrational "pleasure." And that is why the work of Wilhelm Reich is so very important to us all. Certain pleasures further living Life; they help the pulsation of the biological, organismic Orgone energy. Such pleasure is rational—that is, *healthy*. Most of man's "pleasures" are really substitutes for the real thing, or they are run-aways *from* the real thing. We run away because we cannot tolerate real, deep pleasure. And why can't we tolerate real, deep pleasure? Reich showed why. He showed it in many of his books: *The Function of the Orgasm, Character Analysis, The Murder of Christ:* because of patriarchal, sex-negating education at home, in school, in society, the human animal becomes "armored." He develops chronic muscular rigidities which prevent him from feeling his basic emotions of love, anxiety,

9

or anger. He cannot express these basic emotions. He loves
what he should hate and he hates what he should love, or
he is forever running away. Running from whom? From
himself, from being in touch with Life and Love. He runs
from God, which is the basic power that keeps him alive.
Then he kills God in himself, his wife, his children, his pets,
in Nature herself. This is madness. And so you have in-
herited a mad world which is on the brink of extinction.

The other article I read was about two young men who
set a new world's record on the seesaw. They kept the
seesaw in motion for something like 25 days. There, too, is
madness, but of a milder sort. Most politicians keep seesaws in motion for years, decades. They go up and down,
up and down. It's all motion but no progress. It's fine for a
5- or 6-year-old kid to get on a seesaw and go up and
down for a few hours. But armored man never gets off his
seesaw. He constantly vacillates between irrational anxiety
and irrational hatred—back and forth. And that's the basis
for the world's madness—*irrational anxiety*. How do we get
off this abominable seesaw that forever takes society up and
down or Right and Left, but gets us nowhere? How do we
get rid of our constant anxiety, that electric battery that
keeps churning in your guts and gives you no peace? How
do we *discharge* that excess biological, Orgone energy so
we can relax and attend to our necessary business? That is
the problem—the real problem.

Orgastic discharge is the regulating function of excess
biological energy. By orgastic discharge I don't mean
"screwing," I don't mean "laying" or "making it." Most
men and women are impotent. They've got to screw or be
screwed—rape or be raped. They equate sexual intercourse
with defecation. Look at the dirty words scrawled on toilet
walls: they all have to do with armored man's attitude
toward sexuality.

The orgastically potent person can love *fully*, with full,

deep pleasure. He doesn't run around screwing every woman he sees, real or fantasied. He is open, direct, and to the point. He can concentrate on any rational task at hand, because he's not bogged down by the pressures of undischarged Life Energy.

Read the book *Man in the Trap* by Dr. Elsworth F. Baker.° He has put it all on paper, simply and beautifully. But ARM (armored man) won't read Baker or Reich, they disturb him too much. ARM prefers seesaws, the fake movement, so he gets a bit of substitute pleasure, not real pleasure.

The problem is to Let Life Live, so that it can function fully, wholly, and not get stuck in armor in the first place. That's the problem. And it starts with mothers, infants, and children. It involves all of us.

Pulsatory movement is the basis of all pleasure. And *what does the moving?* What senses the movement? Our Life Energy, the Orgone. Place your hands palm to palm and leave them there. First you'll feel your hands, but after a while you will not feel anything, or only very little. Now stroke one palm very gently with the fingertips of the other hand—there is movement and pleasure. The energy field of one hand is interacting with the energy field of the other; the movement enhances the excitation. If you could excite your energy field sufficiently it will glow—it will luminate, as Reich called it. This glow can be measured at Reich's Orgone Energy Field Meter. Reich made pioneering photographs of the excited energy field of the palms. Nobody mentions it—that was some 30 years ago. Nobody mentions it. Why?

We will get to the "whys" later on.

Now, when you're attracted to somebody, your energy field and her energy field are excited. You touch, you stroke,

°New York, Avon, 1974.

right? You continue to touch gently and stroke gently—
and the fields are stimulated to greater excitation, to the
point of glowing. Then you want to *merge* your fields, to
melt, to flow and stream into each other. The two fields
superimpose in mutual, gentle merging, which may or may
not lead to the full genital embrace and orgasm.

Compare what I have just described with what generally
passes for "making love." You see it all the time on TV
or the movies: The guy is panting, wild-eyed, leering; the
girl is busting out of her britches, practically drawing a
bullseye on her vagina, so the guy can "shoot" her; or she
claws and bites and kicks in a pretense of "passion." It is
all make-believe. And when they are "through" they are
either disgusted, bored, or angry. The guy jumps up, zips
his fly and is off at once after another "lay." The girl re-
paints her face and is ready for the next Joe to prick her
open. And that's supposed to be "love"?

They cannot discharge their excess sexual Life energy.
And they run around the world, forever jumping up and
down upon a million different kinds of seesaws, looking for
"pleasure"? For "release"? When they simply cannot tolerate
such full release, such deep pleasure. And it is precisely
this *undischarged*, stale energy that *motivates* pathological
human behavior. Guys steal thousands of cars each year
in America alone, why? To sell them to make money. Why?
To "get girls" so they can "get pleasure"—pleasure which
constantly eludes them; so they steal still more cars, or TV
sets, or rob banks, or mug or even kill, to get more money
to "get broads and booze." Why? To feel the pleasurable
release which they can never really feel. And so the mess
never ends. We build bigger prisons, employ more policemen; but the mess never stops. Then there's alcohol and
drugs, again, for the exact same reason—to "get pleasure" or
to find relief from the constant, gnawing anxiety which
hangs like a monkey upon the neck of ARM. Still there is
no end to the misery.

And then some robotized madmen decide to "go to war," and armored man fights in trenches, on the oceans, and in the air, to kill his Enemy. And all the time the Enemy is himself, his own undischarged biological energy that goads and drives him into a fury to seek release.

You don't believe me, do you? You think this is all "much too simplified." You have been thoroughly brainwashed into believing we fight each other for "political" or "socio-economic" reasons. "Life," you say, "is much too complex" for such simple explanations as undischarged biological-sexual energy. Yes, to ARM, everything is complicated. Nothing can be simple and direct, because the muscular armor makes everything complicated. Reich said it, Baker reaffirmed it, and it remains true as long as man is armored: Armored man is orgastically impotent. He cannot tolerate rational pleasure. He was not born that way, he is made that way. We have got to stop caging mankind in armor, otherwise we shall never get off our huge, crazy, costly, and worthless World Seesaw!

PROJECTION

I have said it before, and, perhaps by the time you are finished listening to me, you will begin to believe me: Armored man is quite mad.

And there lies the greatest pitfall of decent human beings. Oh, yes, we have many, many decent human beings in the world. But they do not know themselves yet. They have no identity, no idea of their value. It is they who make the world go round, who provide the bread and butter and take out the garbage, and fix the toilet when it is broken. But the madmen—ARM—are in control, because *power* and parasitism are their twin engines, driving themselves and our planet to dust.

But the good and decent man, Genital Man, thinks he is nothing, has been made to think he is nothing, and has lost self-confidence in his ability to work, to rule himself and his world. Genital Man hasn't yet learned how to combat ARM. He doesn't realize, for example, that ARM *stinks,* literally. ARM is filled with filth, with filthy thoughts, filthy desires, and filthy obsessions. ARM constantly projects such filth upon Genital Man, he always looks for the *worst* in Genital Man. And if the "worst" is simply not there, then ARM will invent the worst.

On the other hand, Genital Man looks upon ARM as Genital Man, and is therefore always getting slapped in the face or spat upon. Just as the evil person always projects evil, the good person projects the good and expects that all people will act like good people. And this is the great good fortune of ARM and the rotten backwash that always engulfs Genital Man.

If we expected nothing but shit from Armored Man we would never be disappointed. As it is, Genital Man is forever being disappointed, because he cannot believe, to this day, that ARM is so deeply warped. When Genital Man looks at a man in a captain's uniform or a judge's robe or a prelate's garb, he sees the uniform, the robe, the garb, and he projects *beyond* these trappings his idealized image of what "captain," "judge" and "prelate" *should* be. He still cannot conceive of the fact that a criminal, a murderer, or a traitor can live and breathe within the uniform, the robe, or the prelate's garb. He doesn't pay attention to the *emotional expression* behind the façade. Why? Partly out of reluctance to touch the evil, to see it, to smell it, to acknowledge its existence.

ARM has no such reluctance, since he has lived with the evil smell of Deadly Orgone energy (DOR) for many, many years. ARM has no compunction whatsoever against throwing handfuls of dirt upon good people. He does it openly, publicly, before millions. We recall the mock "trials" aimed at making recalcitrant idealists "recant" before the Moscow Masters of Deceit. Genital Man knows it is all a hoax, a mockery, a travesty of justice; but few speak up. Why? Because of a détente with the Moscow Masters? Can one have a détente with a ravaging hyena? Can one have a détente with a rattlesnake? Can a dolphin live in "peaceful coexistence" with a killer shark? This is true madness, true insanity. But just calling it "madness and insanity" doesn't get us anywhere.

And so we invite these Masters of the Emotional Plague to participate in our "EXPO '74" in Spokane, Washington. We extend the hand of friendship to "men" who have imprisoned and slaughtered countless millions for no greater crime than disagreeing with the Plague Masters. I say we *invite* them. Why? Because we don't want to rock the boat? What boat? The business boat? The international politicking boat? The balance-of-powers boat? What boat?

If you have a neighbor who beats up his wife every night and blackens the eyes of his daughter and breaks the arms of his son, do you invite him to dinner because you're afraid he might get angry with *you*? Yes, you will do that, won't you? Secretly you will tell your wife or your husband what a sonofabitch that sadistic bastard really is, but then you will invite him for dinner, won't you? You do that very thing—or, you make excuses by saying, "Well he's a good businessman, a very *big* account, and I wouldn't want to jeopardize that account." That's what you say, on a personal basis, a national basis, and an international basis.

On the street you see your sadistic neighbor wearing a nice white shirt, an expensive suit and tie. His shoes are shined. So you make excuses for him. Anybody who can wear such expensive suits and ties, such nice clean shirts and shiny shoes simply cannot be *that* bad. Besides, he always nods and smiles at you in the street, saying, "Good morning," and smiling. And when he passes you catch a whiff of his expensive after-shave lotion. Any man who wears such expensive after-shave lotion simply couldn't be that bad, could he?

Then you see the wife with bruises on her arms; the daughter with a black eye, and the son with his arms in plaster casts, and for a brief moment the anger surges inside your guts. But you turn your eyes."*Maybe they deserved it?*" you tell yourself. Maybe the wife is a whore, the daughter takes dope, and the son is a thief? You blot out the sight of the bruised and battered faces, just as you blot out the thought of six million people in Africa and India dying of drought, starving on your planet . . . dying. It's not your problem. It's too much—let the "authorities" take care of it.

And that is how you lose your manhood or womanhood—you once-Genital Man and Woman. First you sell yourself and your God out; yes, you sell out, in the little ways; then the bigger sellouts are easier. And, finally, when you crawl your way up to "Success," you have no qualms about inviting vipers and vermin to sit at your table, to make jokes and laugh in their presence, to forget the mountain of skulls and pools of blood and tears that are the backdrops and foundations of what they represent. You break bread with evil and it doesn't sicken you anymore. From now on your projection apparatus is totally out-of-kilter: it only projects in two colors, gold and silver, and the sound track carefully erases any sounds of weeping in the background.

THE EXISTENCE OF HEAVEN

The desire for justice is the strongest argument for the existence of Heaven. Perhaps that is one reason why the

Emotional Plague always tries to stamp out any serious religious belief. The idea of Heaven springs from two sources: Man's impenetrable miseries on earth, and simultaneously those few moments of innocent joy and delight which give him glimpses of a far better existence.

Many believe that there is no such thing as Heaven, and they point to our mundane miseries, arguing, "What God in 'Heaven' would permit such abominations?" The error lies in extrapolating from man to God, and not from God to man. Until we better understand what God is, in practical terms, we can never know what "He" desires or does not desire for his creations. The ancient religionists are indeed correct in attributing man's sorry lot to wide deviations from the Laws of God. Illness, corruption, sloth, cheating, lusting for flesh and power are truly aberrations, products of ARM, not of God. To reacquire Heaven on Earth we must rediscover how we strayed from Heaven into Hell, how we lost our lovely Paradise through sexual pathology. There is a wider, higher game going on in the Cosmos than Earthman is aware of. The twentieth century is much like the fifteenth century, when Columbus opened the route to a New World. Reich opened the route beyond gravity, beyond our limited orb that spins like a tiny jewel in an infinite palace of diadems. By plumbing the depths and heights of human existence, Reich broke through the maze and trap of ARM's own making.

If we can survive as a species these most threatening years; if we can quench the hellfire of the atom in the glow of the cosmic orgone! if we can somehow learn to stop destroying God, who is Love and Life in each newborn child; if we can understand that every living life is a part of the Whole of Life—perhaps we may survive to reach our Heaven. In no age of written history has Man ever faced such decisive alternatives.

ROSES WITHOUT THORNS

Scarcely a week goes by when I do not read some current article, paper, or newsstory detailing a discovery of "momentous import" dealing with some aspect of Reich's discovery of the orgone energy. Yet, Reich and his long labors are scarcely mentioned, if at all. They are photographing "bioplasma," sharpening razor blades with "pyramid energy," seeing auras through "aura goggles," diagnosing illnesses by way of Kirlian photographs. Gnats nibbling at a dead lion. But they are still frightened to death of the dead lion.

Now we read excited accounts of "body language" (stolen from Reich's *Character Analysis*), of encounter groups where one learns to experience *contact* (pilfered from the same source), of psychiatrists who help you "become unified" by "releasing the bio-energy" (they are too gutless to say what they *really* mean—to wit, they will *mobilize* your muscular armor in an effort to bring about orgastic potency).

A thief is someone who takes and uses what is not his own and does so without proper permission or without giving proper credit. Why don't they mention Reich? In many cases they are simply cowards. Reich went to jail and died there for his discoveries; he is therefore still not "accepted." Instead of being *proud* and full of praise for such a man, they are *embarrassed!* The FDA persecution of Reich doesn't embarrass them; the burning and banning of Reich's magnificent works doesn't embarrass them; the strangulation of scientific research in the United States of America doesn't embarrass them. They act as though it were *Reich's fault* that he dared to fight for Truth and Fact! Instead of identifying with the man of Truth and Honor, they identify with the persecutor!

But still the dead lion fascinates them, frightens them, makes them quiver with mixed delight and terror. So they knock out a tooth to wear on a gold chain, or they clip off a claw or snip a piece of the lion's tail. They cannot touch the *whole* Truth for the same reason that they are cowardly hyenas: "To touch truth is to touch the genitals," Reich stated. And they cannot touch their genitals without shame and guilt. The way they avoid Reich's name and work is a dead giveaway to their own orgastic impotence. They want a nice "safe, spruced-up, refined Reich," not a roaring, bounding lion. Everything about Reich's work scares and embarrasses the hell out of them. First of all Reich was what they, in a million years, can never be: A true, 14-carat-gold Genius! That makes them cringe with envy. They hate him for his discoveries of the character armor, of orgastic potency, of bions, of *The Cancer Biopathy*, *The Function of the Orgasm*, his knowledge of *The Murder of Christ*, his unmasking of the Emotional Plague. So they pluck a tiny hair from the end of his lionesque work (a hair surely will never be missed or be seen) and they run to this convention or that symposium and hold up the dead, rootless hair and proclaim it as "My latest discovery!"

But they *are* seen; and we who see it are truly, honestly embarrassed for them— for they are cowardly and small, and sickening in their meanness. They give as another in their endless excuses for theft that Reich was *insane!* To Reich's enemies, he was just as "insane" when he wrote the *Function of the Orgasm* as he was when he wrote *Contact with Space.* If the carcass of a lion is rotten it is *all* rotten, from claws to teeth. But each hyena bites off a bit of hair or tail which in some miraculous way, separated from the whole lion carcass, is suddenly *not* rotten!

But they do not fool us; and they cannot fool themselves. Once they've tasted lion flesh they want more, and still more lion flesh. To touch truth is to desire more truth.

This is an inexorable process. So, one day, when they think no one is looking, they will sneak up on the dead lion and grab a large mouthful of neck, or heart, or genitals, and if they do not simply choke to death, they will burst from the pressure of biting off too much lion.

Reich didn't speak in terms of Lions and Hyenas, but of Roses and Thorns, of those who would steal his lovely roses without accepting the thorns that he suffered to cultivate them.

So we watch this slow, sneaky process of intellectual cannibalism. We remember Reich's marvelous, strong, determined face, his pain and suffering. And we guard his truth and his love-given labors. And we do not forget. We must never forget.

DR. F. A. MESMER*

Franz Anton Mesmer was a very great physician and human being. He was born in 1734 and died in 1815. It was my fate to bridge the centuries between Mesmer and Reich. Until I came along, everyone considered Mesmer "the father of hypnotism." I read a book, *Mind Explorers* by Bromberg and Winkler, and became very interested in Mesmer. I read everything I could find *about* Mesmer; that was exactly like reading what most writers today say *about* Reich. If one wants to study Christianity, don't talk to so-called Christians—*read Christ's words!* The same is true for Reich and Orgonomy. One must go to the *source*, to the roots of things. I've always taught my students to do just that. Don't take anyone's opinion on anything that may have

---

*See my book *Animal Magnetism and the Life Energy*, Exposition Press, 1974.

deep significance—that goes for my opinion, too. We are all subject to bias and error. So, when I read *about* Mesmer I got excited, even though the majority of writers considered him a quack and a charlatan. This was around 1955, after I had undergone orgone therapy and had done enough experimental verification to know in my heart that Reich's discovery of the orgone was factual—*for me!*

I went to the Public Library on 42nd Street and Fifth Avenue in New York City. I spent many hours there, in the third-floor reading room. One day I came across a catalog card indicating Mesmer had written a Memoir in 1799. I obtained a copy. It was in French, as Mesmer had written it. (Mesmer's native tongue was German, although he spoke and wrote French fluently.) I didn't know French, and I couldn't take the book out of the library—it was too precious. My wife and I took our last $17 and obtained a photostatic copy of that book. I later bought French dictionaries and grammar books and spent the next year translating the book. I was a very poor French student in college, so much so that my professor advised me, after two awful semesters, to take Spanish. I did even worse in Spanish. There was no incentive to learn; the courses were required at that time.

Now I had the incentive. Some days I could only translate a few sentences, some days perhaps a paragraph or two. I was thrilled by the concepts of Mesmer. He had stumbled upon the Life Energy, although he called it the "Universal Fluid." Illness was a manifestation of the blockage of the Universal Fluid in the body. The blockage occurs through chronic muscular contractions. I couldn't believe my eyes. I wept and laughed for joy, pacing the floor and struggling with the 18th-century French. Mesmer had invented a "tub" for *accumulating* the Life Energy; he devised a "dry tub" and a "wet tub," very similar to Reich's orgone accumulator and DOR-buster.

Mesmer named his treatment "Animal Magnetism." He

wished to preserve the magnetic (i.e., attractive) nature of his therapy in the word "magnetism," but by calling it "*animal*" magnetism, he wished to show that it was magnetism specifically for *living (anima)* bodies, as opposed to iron or mineral magnetism.

What Mesmer was never able to do was to scientifically objectify his discovery. He was too deeply steeped in mechanism, and science had not progressed far enough to make available the required basic instrumentation.

The hateful world of the emotional plague descended upon Mesmer, just as it descended upon and destroyed Reich 200 years later. The parallels in plague behavior are stunning. I dealt with that subject in my article, "The Emotional Plague Versus Animal Magnetism," published in *The Journal of Orgonomy* (Vol. 1, Nos. 1 and 2, 1967).

No one would publish the translation I had made—no one. This was around 1955. Reich was still very much alive, and I wanted to get Mesmer's words published, believing in my innocence that it might somehow change the climate of opinion surrounding Reich and Orgonomy. In 1956 I bought a hand printing press and fonts of type, and I took a correspondence course in printing. Reich was imprisoned by the time I was proficient enough to begin typesetting the book. He died November 3, 1957. I had just completed binding the first copies of *Memoir of 1799.*

After Mesmer's death in 1815, few scientists were brave enough to openly advocate Animal Magnetism. Around the middle of the 19th century, Dr. John Elliotson of London began publishing a journal dealing with "mesmeric" phenomena. The journal was called *The Zoist.* Elliotson was a brave and valiant physician. He was dismissed from the University Hospital in London for practicing Animal Magnetism, just as Dr. Elsworth Baker was dismissed from an American hospital for practicing orgonomic methods. *The Zoist* was published for about twelve years, carrying many interesting case histories submitted by physicians through-out the world.

Another name that should not be forgotten is Dr. James Esdaille, a contemporary of Elliotson, who practiced Animal Magnetism in India. He performed hundreds of major surgical operations using nothing but Animal Magnetism as anesthetic. His success was so phenomenal that his scientific brethren took every opportunity to stab him in the back.

If you will read the actual work of Mesmer, Elliotson and Esdaille, you will see at once that hypnotism has nothing whatsoever to do with Mesmer's basic principles or procedures. Mesmer used his hands, his fingertips, to convey the Universal Fluid to his patients' bodies. Every cure was accomplished by *a crisis.* Today, in orgonomic language, we would call it a "breakthrough." The energy builds up sufficiently to break through the chronic muscular contractions, or the armor is mobilized enough to permit the energy to flow through the muscular blocks.

After Mesmer's death, others came along and started snipping bits and pieces from his work without acknowledgment. One such was the Baron Charles Von Reichenbach, a German chemist, discoverer of creosote. He claimed Mesmer's work as his own discovery and renamed the Universal Fluid the "Odic Force."

Mesmer's basic work warrants serious consideration, as I believe it holds the key to much of what is called "extrasensory perception" today. Many of Mesmer's patients became somnambulant. They would fall into what Mesmer called a "critical sleep," wherein they could see, hear, taste, and touch with incredibly heightened sensibility. Mesmer never used verbal, suggestive techniques. He made "passes" with hands and fingertips over his patient's body, "communicating" the Universal Fluid to his patient thereby. This is precisely what Christ did with his strong orgone-energy field. The day will come when mankind will understand "miraculous healing" in terms of the movement, lumination, and superimposition of the Life Energy. I do believe we can *direct* this energy with thought. The emotional plague will try to "control" mankind by way of *forcing* behavior and making slaves of humanity. Hypnotism is a perverted off-shoot of Mesmer's discoveries. The emotional plague would like nothing better than to push a button or *will a command* and have millions of people do a jig or fall on their faces. Will another command, and everybody starts working; another command, and we all stop working and fall asleep; another command and we bow down and shout "Hail, Big Brother, King of the World!" Reich unmasked this lust for power, this perversion of Truth and Decency.

The History of Armored Man is the History of the Murder of Life. I am giving you a crash course in self-preservation. Dig yourself deep, factual roots, and prepare to do battle or be enslaved. The face of ARM hasn't changed one expression in 2,000 or 200 years. Read Christ; read Mesmer; read Reich!

ATHEISM

I never met an atheist I could genuinely like—they are more religious in their pose of irreligion than the godliness they hold in contempt. It is impossible to predict how the Children of the Future will act with respect to God, but I suspect they will know God immediately and correctly as the Love-Life in their bodies, as the streaming, pulsating, and luminating orgone energy.

The problem is to guard the Living in infants and children, to safeguard the infant's and child's pulsatory functions. *This means affirming the child's rational genital needs!*

If we do this, then just as the salmon returns to the source of its origin, the genital child will find his way to God.

Homo sapiens of the twentieth century is neither healthy nor rational; therefore, to make judgments based upon sick behavior will lead us deeper into our trap. The atheist has fallen deeply into the trap of muscular armoring, and he cannot get out. So he rages against "God." There is always deep disappointment and heartbreak behind atheism, and also bitter frustration. No atheist could grow in the climate of sexually-affirmative family life. The atheist hates his father or mother—and projects from hatred against Papa to hatred against Our Father. Atheism also is a reaction against having the gospel shoved down one's throat.

What bothers me about atheists is the passionately religious bias they demonstrate when it comes to raising their own children. They'll be damned if *their* kids will be taught about God, or preached to from the Bible in schools or anywhere else! "We don't want our children *indoctrinated* with any religious belief! We want to raise them with *free* minds!" Fine. But the atheist can never raise children with "free" minds, because he must inject into them his *religious anti-religion* of atheism.

I heard an eleven-year-old boy telephone a radio talk-show one night and announce proudly, "I'm an atheist." When asked what his parents were, he replied: "Atheists." And what else? Maybe children who have atheism crammed down their throats will, in later years, become staunch Fundamentalists. It wouldn't surprise me at all. This has happened to many a Communist defector who later embraced Catholicism, and vice versa.

There is a rational and an irrational need to know God. There is a rational need to worship, to give thanks to our Creator, to bless the Giver of Blessings, to revere, to feel humble.

The atheist is the religious rebel. He is a prime example

of how *learning without pleasure* turns into rebellion and hatred. There are two ways to unite the student with any subject: with pleasure or with fear. Most of ARM's learning process takes place through fear: fear of the consequences of failure, fear of what parents might say or do, fear of not getting promoted, fear of social ostracism. *Learning by fear is intellectual rape!* The Life Energy is compliant. Two orgone streams can merge via rape or via genuine love—the product is still matter. But in rape the merger of the orgone streams is *forced, hateful* merging, and a child of this hateful merging is the product. Such a child is never really wanted, never really loved—it is, in short, rejected. A child born of the gentle, loving merger of two orgone streams is wanted, desired, loved. The difference lies in the presence or absence of genuine pleasure during the merging process, and nothing else.

So, too, when we learn with pleasure, we truly love what we learn. When we are forced, by anger or fear, to learn something, we are being raped! And we will reject such learning or rebel against it. Be careful not to confuse the real, self-regulating function of learning with the sly and contrived methods of ARM which use artificial "rewards" in the form of gold stars, names on the Dean's List, or an extra bowlful of rice. Learn a new word and get a cookie is Pavlov's reflex dressed up in academic robes.

We have got to stop indoctrinating children in any isms, any "ists." When I was a kid going to grade school in The Bronx, New York, I met a group of schoolkids on our way to lunch. There was a presidential election coming up, and politics was much in conversation. "What are you?" the kids asked me, "Are you a Republican or a Democrat?" Since my father was a member of the local Republican club, my answer was ordained: "I'm a Republican," I responded proudly. "Well, we're Democrats!" the kids sneered, and began shoving me around. I shoved back, but there were too many of them. When I got home for lunch, my mother noticed my scratched and dirty face and my torn clothes. When I told her what happened, she said, "Next time, when you're outnumbered, tell them you're a Democrat."

On my return to school, I was stopped by another group of kids who also wanted to know my political stand. "I'm a Democrat," I said. As it turned out, this group embraced the Republican platform, so I was soundly trounced a second time.

That night I discussed these events with my father. He shook his head. "The next time they ask you what you are, tell them you're an Independent."

The following morning I was in the schoolyard when a third group of kids demanded to know my political affiliation. "I'm an Independent," I said warily, whereupon I was pushed and shoved and thrown to the ground, my hat was stomped, and my books strewn all over. "What the hell's an 'Independent'? Are you a wise guy?" the gang leader yelled in my ear.

A few days later my father brought home a punching bag and two pairs of boxing gloves. "If you're going to live in this world, it's time you learned how to fight," he said. My father was an excellent boxer. He taught me something practical, useful, and necessary; and he taught it to me at a time when I needed it.

Almost a half-century is gone. I still greatly admire my father. And I'm still totally apolitical.

PURRING AND PLEASURE

"If you play with cats you will go crazy." That was a dictum injected into me as a child growing up in a sex-negating environment. Thus I developed a terrible fear and fascination for cats. Occasionally I would take a kitten on my lap and stroke its soft, warm body, and I would hear and feel the streamings of life energy moving in that body —and my own life energy would stream through my genitals. The purrings of pleasure in cat and man are functionally identical. But the purring in the cat and my body would frighten me: It would make me crazy.

The taboo against pleasure itself starts very early—in infancy, and perhaps even earlier. ARM cannot tolerate the purring of the Life Energy. He will go "mad" if he touches his genitals.

What is health and happiness to Genital Man must, perforce, be "madness" to ARM. We solve nothing by simply dismissing ARM's irrationality as "madness" itself. We are obliged to find the Truth in such madness, if we wish to change the way things have always been.

Real pleasure always involves the genitals; however, ARM has been cut off completely from deep genital contact, deep pleasure. He can stand *little* movements, bits and pieces of pleasure, but he cannot tolerate deep and high waves of pleasure. He can look at a painting in a frame in a museum, but he cannot stand the face of raw, unframed, unhoused Nature herself—in mountain, field, or sea. As soon as he finds himself alone in raw, unframed Nature, ARM pulls out a transistor radio or a portable TV set, and turns them on. He can find "peace" in the dismal isolation of a city, cut off from anything green, alive, and pulsating, but he feels lost and alone in the infinite joys of the wilderness. And this is part of ARM's terrible tragedy.

When I could love with pleasure—finally, I could stroke a cat, too, without guilt; and I could find love in good work. The ability to love fully is the foundation of all good, all goodness, and all greatness. That is why we must guard the Ways of Love in infants and children. If the capacity to give and receive love is twisted, thwarted, or destroyed— nothing else can save us, nothing!

Of course, if our genitality is crippled too severely, we must seek help. We must break out of our armor. And we cannot do this alone. We need the best professional help, so we find a qualified medical orgone therapist. I said a "qualified medical orgone therapist." Now that orgonomy is becoming "accepted," many have jumped onto the bandwagon and are calling themselves "orgone therapists." Or they will claim they are using Reich's *Character Analysis* as the basis of their therapy. Be careful. Be sure. Don't trust your life to an incompetent or an irresponsible person.

HOMOSEXUALITY—THE DANGEROUS EQUATION

On December 16, 1973, newspapers throughout the United States carried a news release from the American Psychiatric Association stating that the Association's board of trustees voted 13 to 0 to remove homosexuality from the category of psychiatric disorders. No longer is homosexuality to be considered an "illness." The news release stated:

> The trustees are the policy-making board of the 20,000-member American Psychiatric Association. They also approved a three-part resolution putting the association on record as:
> —Urging the repeal of laws in 42 states and the District of Columbia "making criminal offenses of sexual acts performed by consenting adults in private."
> —Deploring public and private discrimination against homosexuals in employment, housing, public accommodations and licensing.
> —Urging enactment of laws at all levels to "insure homosexual citizens the same protection now guaranteed to others."

To equate homosexuality with "health" is as erroneous as it is weird. It speaks volumes about the trustees of the APA. I read somewhere that the highest incidence of suicides among medical doctors occurs to psychiatrists. This is not surprising. No armored medical doctor enters medicine for rational reasons. Most who become psychiatrists are seeking answers to their own emotional problems. And I hate to think about the damage being done by armored pediatricians to the newborn.

But I was discussing homosexuality. No farmer, cattle-man, or rancher would consider a homosexual horse, sheep, or pig to be "healthy." But, of course, no farmer, cattleman, or rancher has had the advantages of educational brain-washing which turns things upside down and inside out. Homosexuals exercise considerable influence in all civilized societies, in the arts, the news media, and in politics. Homo-sexuality could not flourish in a sex-affirmative society, no more than malnutrition could exist in a well-fed community. Whenever an individual is deprived of the normal hetero-sexual outlets, homosexuality is seeded. In the Navy, during World War II and during the Korean War, I watched homo-sexual relationships develop aboard ship. The longer we remained at sea, the greater the spread of homosexuality.

No homosexual prefers his or her life by way of a rational choice, freely made and freely given. It is the old tale of the fox who lost his tail (genitals). He can only pretend that a tail-less existence is preferable. As I have said in *Planet in Trouble,* I am not "against" homosexuality, any more than I am "against" tuberculosis or cancer. Two con-senting adults should have a right to live their lives un-molested in private. But I am relentlessly against homo-sexuals in any professions where they come into prolonged influential contact with children—especially in education. Until the child becomes able to run his own life as a respon-sible person, he must be protected from harmful influences, be they rattlesnakes, Red or Black Fascists or those suffer-ing from a perversion. I am also opposed to the public flaunting of homosexuality, just as I would be against chil-dren visiting insane asylums.

The strong influence of homosexuality upon society is

derived from the *consciousness of the importance of sexuality*. When the organism is *conscious* of its sexual needs and gratifications (however perverted they may be) there must be a strong life-drive to begin with. This accounts for the fact that many "great" men and women were homosexuals. They were able to "drink from the Waters of Life" despite the mud in the water. As Reich stated: "Dirty water is better than no water at all." But the homosexuality itself was not the underlying cause of the "greatness," as homosexuals would have us believe. A one-armed sculptor may be great; but how much greater would he have been with two arms?

I would prohibit—that is, I would make it illegal—for homosexuals to have children. Homosexuals point out, correctly, that many so-called heterosexuals are cruel and perverse parents. This is very true. I think the responsibility of parenthood is taken too lightly in general. Someday, perhaps, we will have Parenthood Boards, comprised of orgonomically oriented physicians and sociologists who will pass upon the parental qualifications of men and women.

The fact that homosexuality is an illness is verified in Reich's clinical findings: Cf. *Character Analysis*. Sexual aberrations are functionally identical with chronic muscular rigidities (character armoring). It is interesting that those with sexual aberrations are referred to as "inverts" and "perverts." What, one should ask, is "inverted" or "perverted" if not the biological energy itself? Instead of flowing naturally to the genital area, the orgone is shunted and twisted by the armor—hence the emotional feeling of inversion or perversion has a biological and physiological basis in the "perversion" of the Life Energy itself. I've often wondered if the expressions "Leftist" and "Rightist" similarly describe strong deflections of the biological orgone in the body. I leave it to you new students in orgonomy to supply the answers.

A CHILDREN'S LIBERATION MOVEMENT*

Everyone seems to be joining a liberation movement. We have a Black Liberation movement, a Women's Liberation movement, a Gay Liberation movement, another for Indians, Chicanos, and now we have a Men's Liberation movement to counteract the Women's Liberation movement. Apparently the women want to be "liberated" from male domination and the men want to be liberated from female domination. How did all this *loss* of liberty happen in the first place?

Since it takes a male and a female to reproduce (and, in most cases, raise) a child—certainly *both men and women* must have participated in the loss of liberty, must have actively or passively affirmed and encouraged such loss of liberty. Since, moreover, our liberties must somehow have been lost in childhood, it would seem that only in childhood can they be safeguarded. But nobody mentions that. The Blacks are for Blacks; women are for women; homosexuals are for the right to be homosexuals. But nobody stands up for the Rights of the Child. Because the human infant and child represent the common denominator of *all* future "movements," wouldn't it be prudent to insure that the rational liberties accorded by God to mankind in infancy shall be affirmed, protected, and furthered throughout childhood, adolescence, and adulthood?

I therefore propose a worldwide "Children's Liberation Movement"—a movement that will strive to guarantee to *every* Earthchild the Right to Life, Love, Knowledge, and Rational Work. (When I say "rational," I mean any act or pursuit that conforms to Truth and Fact, or seeks to study

---

*Reprinted with permission from my article in *Caveat Emptor*, April, 1974.

and disseminate New Truth and Fact.) But, you might ask, don't children have certain rights at the present time?

No, they do not. As a group, children are the single most oppressed people in the world. I speak now of *all* children, white, black, red, or yellow. Because they are the weakest specimens of *homo sapiens*, children can neither defend themselves against anti-Life measures, nor petition for a redress of grievances. They cannot fight against, speak against, or legislate against any one of a number of oppressive measures to which, from birth (and even before birth) they are subjected. Let us look at only a few of some of these anti-life measures which the majority of the world's children experience.

First—every infant begins his or her existence as an organism dwelling within the mother's womb for approximately 270 days and nights. In this protected environment (we are of course assuming the mother is fairly healthy) the organism feeds, eliminates, and moves and develops autonomically. Also, in this protected, warm and secure environment—*in constant bioenergetic contact with the mother*—the organism carries on a totally self-regulated existence. Suddenly, one day it is "born." From an environmental temperature of, say, 98.6 degrees, the infant finds itself thrust into a room considerably colder; and it is naked. Suddenly, too, it feels itself grasped by both ankles and lifted unceremoniously upside down, while simultaneously being smacked across its bottom by the hand of the attending nurse or physician. "Welcome, *homo sapiens*, to your new world!" My friend, Dr. Oscar Tropp, who was both a pediatrician and an orgone therapist, remarked: "Every animal licks its newborn with the tongue; but only Man 'licks' its newborn with the hand!"

Okay—what happens next to our "liberated" infant? The doctor or nurse squirts silver nitrate into its eyes! Silver nitrate (in case you don't remember) burns like hell in the delicate tissues of the eyes! Yes, I know, silver nitrate is supposed to prevent any gonococcus infection in the eyes. But there is a simple, inexpensive and quick test that could be run on the mother which would easily determine whether she has or hasn't got a gonococcus infection. Such a test takes only a few minutes. But the hospitals don't routinely run those tests—better to squirt acid into the wide-open, unarmored eyes of every single newborn baby!

Now, what subsequent "liberation movement" is our infant favored with? The baby is *routinely removed from its mother!* Why? we ask. "Because that's the way it is done all over the civilized world," we are told. But why is the baby deprived of the important bodily, energetic contact with its mother; and why isn't it allowed to breast-feed at birth? "Because that's the way we do things," is the reply —"and mind your own impertinent business!" (Having spent over six years in the hospital field, and having visited nearly every major hospital in the United States—and some in Canada—I am convinced that most hospitals are run for the convenience of the staff, not for the patients, and certainly not for helpless infants!)

All right—so here we have our new "liberated" infant, male or female, black, white or green. All, *all* are routinely "liberated" by being yanked upside down and rump-slapped at birth, given a squirt of eye-liberating silver nitrate in the eyes, removed from energetic bodily contact with the mother, then placed (usually swaddled so that they can't "scratch themselves" in clothing so tightly binding as to restrict all movement) in a roomful of pitifully screaming babies. And there the infant remains, not to be fed a mouthful until the hospital timetable says each one may eat! Is this "liberation" or oppression and deprivation of the cruelest kind? And from this type of horror mankind expects to develop "liberated" adults?

But wait, we are by no means finished with our timetable of terrors. As Reich so aptly described these barbarities in his stunning article, "The Source of the Human 'No'," the next generalized torment is reserved for male infants. Routinely, the next step in our scenario of "liberation" is to cut off the tip of the male's most sensitive organ—the infant is circumcised. Why? we ask again. "Shut up!" we are told. "The kid might develop trouble later on with his foreskin. It's a preventative measure!" So why not remove the adenoids, the appendix, maybe a kidney, and give him an artificial heart at the same time? Certainly the kid "might develop" trouble with these organs, too! Why subject each male child to the barbarism of circumcision?

Born into a cold world, yanked upside down, slapped on the bottom, removed from its mother, unable to feed at will, unable to move, and then to feel the knife of the physician on its genital organ—that's the beginning of the Murder of Life on our planet. And as Reich said, armored man doesn't hear or see or feel this continuous murder. He gets all upset if one child falls down a well; thousands will express concern, will rush to help. But the widespread Murder of Life evokes no protests. And from this ritualized, institutionalized beginning we wish to raise "healthy, happy, liberated adults"?

Then the child grows up, reaching puberty. This is the period of increasing genital pressure, the build-up of the natural rhythm of Life Energy. Society, however, offers no rational, socially-approved way of dealing with *natural* (rational) heterosexual needs. The youngster is constantly warned against "touching himself." Why? How does a child find relief from the goading pressures of an increasing sexual development? The sexual energy and the Life Energy are functionally identical. Kill the sexuality of a child and you kill the child's life. But the parents constantly warn the adolescent: "Don't masturbate or you'll form bad habits. Don't have intercourse or I'll break your neck! And if you

should have a child I'll disown you or throw you in jail!"
What then can the adolescent do? Play ball? Take cold
showers? No amount of track meets or cold showers can
bring the discharge of sexual energy which the adolescent
organism requires. So what, in fact, does the adolescent do?
We know by our juvenile delinquency statistics precisely
what they do. They start drinking, or taking drugs, or steal-
ing cars (so they can be alone with each other), or they
run away from home and become hippies or yippies or God
knows what. And who can blame them?

If an adolescent cannot express his or her *God-given*
genital love, then this love will eventually become distorted,
perverted and vicious. Or the youngster will simply *resign*.
And *chronic resignation*, as Reich showed in his book *The
Cancer Biopathy*, is the seedbed of cancer.

Is it any wonder that so many youngsters, at the height
of their sexual need, commit suicide? Is it any wonder that
homosexuality is so rampant? Actually, society *prefers* the
sickness of homosexuality to the healthy development of
heterosexual adults! A person who is chronically denied a
natural outlet for expressions of love must eventually become filled with either hatred (he or she becomes "de-
linquent") or become resigned to illness and death.

Where, therefore, is the "Liberation Movement" that
speaks for children? All children. Who guarantees the human infant the right NOT to be molested and physically
oppressed at birth, in childhood, and adolescence? Who
speaks for the Natural-Lawful Right of the adolescent to
fulfill his or her God-given sexual needs? Who speaks for
the Right of such young people to have proper counseling,
privacy, and the *affirmation* of their natural heterosexual
expressions? Who will affirm the adolescent's right to knowledge and use of contraceptives? If a young girl becomes
pregnant because she is totally ignorant of the process of
birth, or is denied the use of contraceptives, is it she or
society who is really criminally negligent?

But very few—if any at all—will openly affirm these minimum Rights of Young People. The homosexual wants the right to be a homosexual, *in public;* and wants the added "right" to *convert* heterosexuals to homosexuality.°
But not a single word is spoken for the Right of Youth NOT TO BE A HOMOSEXUAL!

Liberationists want the right to be *what?* Liberated? How can a twisted tree suddenly become a straight tree? The miseries of childhood and adolescence are not confined to any single race, religion, or class. Armored humanity, everywhere, in every country, in every school, in every nursery—armored man *per se*—is the recreator of armored, characterologically chained, humanity.

A really radical thinker goes "to the roots" of things. And the human condition does not spring fullblown in adulthood. Man's social miseries and persecutions—*and acquiescence to evil*—can only be stopped precisely where they begin: at birth, in infancy, and in adolescence. Until our pseudo-liberationists are willing to stand up for the Rights of Children and Youth, the so-called Liberation Movements are a sham and a delusion. Such "movements" are in reality an evasion of the essential, the hollow pantomime of the freedom peddler and the quack.

If the natural sexual expressions of children and youth are "immoral, illegal, or unhealthy," then what makes them suddenly, at age 18 or 21, "moral, legal, and healthy"? As the late A. S. Neill said, "Sex that is dirty in the nursery cannot be clean in the marriage bed."

Yes, humanity needs a Liberation Movement—but a *true* liberation movement that strikes at man's deepest illness and irrationality. By focusing attention on the basic Rights of Children and Youths, we shall begin to lay the axe to the very foundations of *all* adult oppression and misery.

°See *Newsweek*, "The Boys in the Band," March 25, 1974, p. 108.

"LOVE" AS DECREED BY BIG BROTHER

Reich was damned by both the Nazis and the Communists, whom he called Black and Red Fascists, respectively. The Far Right and the Far Left are two sides of the same anti-Life coin; they have a common root (a common functioning principle) in their authoritarian, sex-negating attitude, an attitude which extends to all things natural and truly Godly.

There is a great deal that is wrong with the United States of America; but in the latter part of the twentieth century it still offers the greatest amount of individual sexual freedom—and without sexual freedom true democracy is impossible. Now I realize that when I say "sexual freedom," armored man thinks in terms of free-screwing-around without thought of responsibility and decency, of running naked through courtrooms and campuses like a bunch of bratty kids, of shocking and knocking and shouting dirty words. There is a world of difference between the quick fuck and the glowing merger of two loving people in the genital embrace. This difference is not something you can simply talk about or merely describe. It has to be experienced to be known; just like color perception has to be experienced. Reich's work will always be distorted by distorted people who cannot conceive of real natural love, of real responsible mating and lovingness and tenderness between two people. To armored man (and their armored rulers) love is always equated with licentiousness, lust, rape, screwing around and the dirty fuck, all of which must be controlled by the Red or Black Masterminds.

The best way to make any animal submissive is to castrate it. Ask any rancher or cattleman. The most "spirited" animals are those whose capacity and opportunity to mate are given free natural expression. The fascist castrates his children or his society through authoritarian, sex-negating measures in the form of "codes of conduct" or "moral laws." If you ask the Fascist Masters for the scientific reasons behind such "codes" you are apt to get your brains shot out. Besides, when one is brainwashed for the first 18 years of his existence, it is hardly likely that one would have enough life left to even be able to *formulate* such "counter-revolutionary" questions. Rare, indeed, are the Solzhenitsyns; their voices pose a greater threat to the fascist's domain than any real or fantasied nuclear weapons, because they encourage the *freedom of thought!* Radical "root-reaching" thought, and freedom to think as free men are the greatest perils to the Emotional Plague Masters.

Initially, in whatever guise it presents itself, Fascism enchants and entices the masses by way of dangling the carrot of "Liberation of the Masses." Everybody yearns for "freedom" since all are bound in rigid muscular armor. But real, genuine freedom always presupposes a natural, rational, heterosexuality—the ability to express one's genital love in accordance with the laws of Nature and Nature's God. The Russian Revolution rapidly degenerated into the free-fuck-for-all philosophy of permissiveness, pornography and pimpery. The Russian people, already tainted with sex-negative authoritarianism, simply could not fulfill the self-regulating goals that dreamers and schemers dangled before them. Thus, eventually, more rigid and more repressive anti-sexual measures had to be imposed than had existed prior to this very revolution which sought to "liberate" the masses. The lesson was harsh and implacable: *Freedom cannot be imposed; it must be lived from birth!* One cannot "liberate the masses" simply by passing decrees. (See Reich's *The Sexual Revolution.*)

And now we turn to the Peoples Republic of China, the largest mass adventure into fascism in the world's history. Chairman Mao, the Ping-Pong Impresario of the Orient, boasts of the splendidly liberated masses, the increase in Red Chinese productivity, the new schools, universities, theaters, the respect for law and order, the prim morality and industry of the young Red students.

But you, the Students of the Future, should not be hood-winked by the brainwashed idiocy of walkie-talkie prop-agandists. *There is one, and only one, rational measure to use in assessing the amount of "freedom" enjoyed in any country: The amount of rational, natural heterosexuality enjoyed by adolescents and adults. To the degree that na-tural heterosexual expressions are socially affirmed and encouraged, to that degree can one say that "freedom" truly exists. Conversely, to the degree that natural heterosexual expressions are frustrated, banned, condemned, or pro-hibited, to that degree does fascism and the Emotional Plague flourish.*

And so we have only to examine the official Red Chinese attitude toward natural sexuality to understand what is really going on in the bodies and minds of Red Chinese youth. An article, "When Boy Meets Girl in China," by Jan Heemskirk and Theo Van Houts, published in the March 24, 1974 issue of *Parade* gives us the true picture. Any overt display of affection on the part of "unmarried" Chinese males and females is totally taboo, and even "unthinkable." Red Chinese students find "incomprehensible" the idea that Western male and female students often live together before marriage.

One Chinese student expressed himself in this manner: "I don't believe [premarital sexual relationships] is a good thing. We want to study, and that takes all our energy."

To this I say—horsefeathers! First of all, since this student lives under a strict dictatorial system, what would you *expect* him to say! Since Chairman Mao's Little Red Schools with their Little Red Schoolbooks and their Big Red School Guards prohibit in word and deed *any* natural heterosexual expressions, can a "proper Red Student" publicly announce himself *for* sexuality? "We want to study," smiles the Good Little Red Schoolhouse Soldier-in-the-making, "and that takes all our energy."

And another Red Student solemnly states: "In our country young men and women do not think about such things."

And another Red mouthpiece chimes in: "If young men and women live together, then they think only of their own personal happiness, and we do not think that is correct."

Now, let us examine these statements in the light of orgonomic knowledge. Based upon the hundreds of students I have worked with in both public and private schools, I have found that the ability to study and get good grades was in direct proportion to the student's ability to gratify himself *without guilt!* Every single so-called problem student was sexually frustrated. To the degree that I was able to help the student overcome his sexual inhibitons and frustrations, to that degree did his ability to study and work improve!

Anyone who has had the slightest contactful relationship with adolescent and young students knows that sexual tensions and unfulfilled love-needs constitute their single primary interest. If a youngster is hungry, he can only think about food *all the time!* He simply cannot keep his mind on his studies. Of course, society (as occurs in every Red Schoolhouse) can intimidate the student, can brainwash the student, can compulsively "teach" the student, and does so under penalty of punishment, ostracism, or even death.

Studies done in universities in the United States prove that the sexually satisfied student is a better student, able to concentrate upon his or her work without feeling the constant harassment of frustrated love.

But in Red China, the good little Chinese students

politely tell their interviewers that "they never think about" members of the opposite sex! "We never talk about boys," says a Chinese girl candidate for the Red Board of Morality, "why would we?" Then she adds, "If one devotes time to such things, one has no energy left to study." And how, pray tell, would this little Red spinster know *that*? She is simply echoing the litany officially prescribed by the Party. Could she say anything else? Would you expect a devout Hindu to advocate the practice of Protestantism?

But let us listen to this pre-tape-recorded, "spontaneous" outpouring of official student sentiment with respect to sexual intercourse, marriage, and pregnancy: When four Chinese students were asked how many children they wanted to have—wonder of wonders—they *all* replied, "two children." How did it happen that all of the Red Chinese students determined to have but *two* children? "Our leaders say that two children are sufficient, and if that is what our leaders say, that is what we will do. . . . Our first duty is to think of the welfare of our country. If our leaders say we should only have one child, then we have only one; if he says three, we will have three." (Thus speaks Chairman Mao: "If I say *three* children, then, dammit—three it must be, even if it *kills* you!")

"And what do you think of premarital sexual relations?" ask the interviewers. "That is a terrible thing," replies the pre-recorded Red Chinese student.

If you ask her, "Why is premarital sexual relations a terrible thing?" the proper response, of course, is—"It deprives the State of energy." Or, "It is counterproductive." Or, "Sex is only for marriage and children." Or, "One who does so is simply not properly educated and must therefore be reeducated."

To disgress for a moment: I recall that during World War II, any student at the U.S. Naval Academy at Annapolis who was caught masturbating could be summarily dismissed from the Academy. What would you expect a cadet to answer if asked what he thought about masturbation?

Interviewer: All right, mister. What is your attitude toward masturbation by cadets here at Annapolis?

Cadet: It's a deplorable habit, sir, gives evidence of congenital weakness, may lead to insanity or hair on the palms, deprives the cadet of the energy to kill, and is certainly counterproductive, sir.

Interviewer: What do you think of girls, premarital sex, or marriage, mister?

Cadet: I never think about them, sir. I simply never think about them.

BY THE FIRESIDE

Today is March 31, 1974—a severely Dorized day. It has been a severely Dorized winter, with much radioactivity coming over from the West and Southwest. The AEC has announced some 27 radioactive leaks at the Hanford, Wash., radioactive dumping grounds. God alone knows how many *unannounced* leaks they have had and are having.

It is a day of dying today. Difficult to move and to think, to walk or to live. I wonder how much more we can tolerate. "You will move until you cannot move anymore", one medical orgone therapist told me. I took a prolonged, soaking, lukewarm bath to get rid of some of the DOR: that helped. It usually does. Then I drank some wine and built a fire in our fireplace. I've always enjoyed a warm fire on a miserable, contracted day. From my window I see the DOR coming over, continually coming over. Nobody sees it. Nobody mentions it. If they could not touch the orgone for thousands of years, they cannot touch DOR.

So I've spent much time today at the fireside, and I've thought of the Fire of Life and the Fire of Death: the cosmic orgone energy can become either. It depends upon the conditions. The creative Fire of Life streams from the Universe into our solar system, our planet, our bodies. It is the Creative Life Force that builds, nourishes, causes growth, development, thought, art, work, and love. It is "the friendly fire," in the parlance of the insurance business. A fire in one's fireplace is a friendly fire. A fire in the middle of the livingroom rug is not a friendly fire; that's an unfriendly fire, in insurance language.

Under one set of circumstances fire is good, healthful, beneficial; and under another set of circumstances, the same fire becomes a destructive killer, a ruthless destroyer. The sunlight (orgone) in the desert can kill you; in the Arctic the same sunlight stirs matter and life to grow and mate. In a clean and balanced atmosphere the orgone brings life and health and growth. In an atmosphere contaminated by nuclear energy the same orgone becomes oranur, a highly excited killer-type energy—it is all the same orgone energy under different sets of circumstances.

In a healthy body the orgone pulsates, sparkles, streams, and feels good to one's contact with it. In a sick body (i.e., one filled with DOR) the same orgone feels like electricity (maybe it actually *is* converted into electricity), and becomes highly excited and feverish. The fever is the Life Energy's response to the DOR in the organism. Fever is a "living fire" which is the body's way of burning up the DOR, reducing it, trying to get rid of it. Too much fever can kill the sick person; too little fever is not sufficient to do the job. Again we see how the living exists on such a narrow margin of "Life." Too far to either the left or the right and we are in trouble: too much acid, or too much alkalinity; too low or too high a body temperature; too much or too little blood sugar, white and red corpuscles, or any of the chemical constituents. We walk and exist on a very narrow path of "Life" in deed and in fact.

Reich had a really magnificent hope toward the end of his life. He saw the real possibility of actually *extending the Limits of Life,* of broadening the razor's edge upon which life must now exist. This would have meant much less sickness to the human community, and much greater life-spans. This hope of his had to do with his discovery of Oranur and ORUR. He had found a way to mate the unfriendly fire of the atom with the friendly fire of the orgone.

At the present time, Man woos and courts the favor of the atom. He is killing himself, and you and me. How can we stop him? Atomic man represents the greatest killing force on our planet. How do we stop him? He will not listen to reason; he will not even read Reich. He is a killer and he is killing Life on Earth. He is a murderer—a true Enemy of Man, and he should be treated exactly as we would treat any other mad-dog of a murderer. You must make your world in such a way that such Murder and such Murderers *cannot* exist; It is too late for me and my world to do anything about that now. My world *protects* the Murderers and kills the Christs and the Reichs, and the rest of us to boot. It is up to you to *know* Life, to *study* Life, to *protect* Life, to *further* Life. And to do this, you must study the basis of Life itself, the Life Energy. This will help keep you and your world safe and sane.

SO YOU WANT TO TEACH

Teaching children is probably the single most important profession in any society. Christ was a "rabbi," a teacher; he touched truth and he was murdered. It is the most dangerous profession, not because of the children, but because of parents and fellow-teachers. I am talking now of public-school teaching. After I was fired, for the second time, from a public-school payroll (the first time was from a private-school payroll, but there is no essential difference), Dr. Eva Reich wrote me a sympathetic note, saying, "You can't teach truth on a public payroll." She was right.

A. S. Neill advised any potential teacher who really loved children to forget teaching as a career. "Sell pencils instead," was his advice.

Yes, if you love children, if you have deep contact with them and desire to help them grow, you will find only misery and heartache in public schools. To be truly "in touch" with children is to understand their basic genital needs and to affirm and protect those needs. This you cannot do in public schools. The Hounds of Hell will smell you out; they will spy on you and your students; they will accuse you of immoral conduct, and you will be lucky to escape with your skin intact.

I assume here that you are fairly healthy yourself, that you know the difference between freedom and license, that you can touch sexual questions wholesomely and without guilt or hatred. Above all, I assume that your own sexual life is gratifying. Without a happy sex life of your own, you will never be able to touch the high-power of young Life without becoming a Freedom Peddler or a rebel.

Most teachers hate children. They became teachers in the first place because they failed at other things, or because of an irrational desire to "teach," that is, to *suppress* life. You will know such haters-of-Life by their false smiles and the beady, gleaming fire that sparks from their eyes. They are awful, miserable people. They exist by sucking the rich living juices from their students whom they eventually flatten and destroy.

If you enter public-school teaching, within five years

or less you will become bitter and hard. You will have to, or you won't be able to continue. You will be torn apart by your loving contact with children and your desire to help them on one hand, and the emotional plague that is presently stronger than you.

But you don't believe me. You think that conditions have changed in the last 10 or 15 years. You offer as evidence the fact that certain schools are teaching "sex classes" to children, including young children. It is not a matter of "teaching sex," but of *why* they are teaching about sexuality, and *who* is doing the teaching. Sex classes are really disguised courses in anti-sexuality. They do not rationally affirm the child's right to gratify himself; they do not protect the child's right to the genital embrace *when the child is ready for it.* Such sex classes are either too far right or too far left: either puritanical or permissive. Practicing nudity in the classroom, for example, is simply contempt for genitality; it is saying, "See, there's really *nothing* to having a penis or a vagina!" Unhealthy teachers who "teach sex" are really indulging in perverse gratification.

In a truly pro-Life school, one would not have to "teach" sexuality; no more than one has to "teach" a child how to enjoy eating. Questions regarding sexuality would arise naturally and spontaneously in the classroom, and would be dealt with, just as eating and food are dealt with, in a simple, pleasurable manner.

I refer here to your *attitude* toward sexuality. If you are open, straightforward, and relatively unarmored, your students will eventually feel at ease enough to ask you their deepest sexual questions—in their own good time. Yes, it is certainly important to understand the biological functions of the body, to understand the cycle of birth, the role of the genitals in conception. In a healthy family environment, these facts will be known simply as a part of life.

But, in general, the kids in your classroom will not come from healthy environments. They will range from slight to severe armoring; they will sucker you into "saving" them. Then, after you've "discussed" their sexual problems with them, they will run home and tell their parents or their priests about your "dirty sex talks" in the classroom. That's what eventually killed Homer Lane, the great British educator. And that's what nearly got me killed twice.

So what can you do about all this? You could start your own school; and that in itself is not easy. Oh, the actual school incorporation, getting some land, a building, a small staff—those are not impossible. That's relatively simple. But getting the *students*—that's the snake in the succotash! If you can get parents who understand what the sexual health of children involves; if you can get parents to trust the self-regulatory functions of children; if you can get parents to send you their kids, you might have a ghost of a chance.

And that means, also, getting the right teachers. One bad apple will soon ruin your entire program.

Understand that *true sexual health for children is social dynamite!* What will you do when your teenage boys and girls start pairing off and long to love each other in the body? You will have contraceptive problems. You will have, therefore, legal problems and social problems. And you may eventually end up with abortion problems. Your neck will be two-feet out on the chopping block. So, unless you have total social approval, you are a helpless, hopeless target for every sexually crippled and warped killer who gets wind of what's going on at your school.

But you are young and full of life and good dreams. So you will tell me to go to hell, and you will do what you want anyway. That's precisely what I did in your shoes. If you really love children that much and desire to teach, then, of course, you will. And no Neill or Eden will sway you. I'm glad: may God's good luck smile on you—you will need every bit of it.

THE ULTIMATE BARBARITY

I have often told you that a society that suppresses the natural heterosexuality of children will simultaneously affirm sexual perversity. Armored humanity continually castrates its children to conform to standards of armored existence. To know true genital sweetness and pleasure, to glow with natural love for one of the opposite sex—these are considered wrong, immoral, and even "illegal." Parents do not (and in fact cannot) affirm their son's or their daughter's *right* to touch the genitals with full pleasure. They cannot affirm and protect their child's right and rational need to love—in the body—someone of the opposite sex.

Reich's great work shows that our God-given need for sexual gratification occurs long before the reproductive functions are mature, and continues long after the woman is capable of bearing children. Thus, the need to give and receive genital love is *not* a function reserved solely for child-bearing, but, rather, the process of human reproduction is *secondary* to man's basic and primary need to discharge excess bioenergy during the genital embrace.

Since armored man condemns rational genital expressions in children and adolescents, he kills that which should be man's most profoundly pleasurable experience. He kills the *capacity* to experience true love. He perverts real love into a disgusting act of lust, perversion, or depravity. This is the true "Murder of Christ," which every civilized man and woman has experienced.

And thus armored society encourages, condones, fosters,

promotes and makes legal the very "perversions" which it
says it is *against!* This is another example of "rationalized
social insanity."

I said we castrate children—at birth, in the nursery, the
home, the school, and then we hypocritically decry the
amount of perversion in the world. I said we *prefer* the
sick to the healthy. But many of you will not believe me.
You don't want to touch this misery, this human inferno;
you refuse to see it or hear it or believe it. Or, when I say,
"We castrate people," you assume I am speaking meta-
phorically, or you might concede that we do in fact "castrate" human beings "emotionally." You don't realize that
everything . . . *everything* we do begins with the emotions,
with how the orgone moves in our bodies. And therefore
from emotional castration to physical, surgical castration is
no more than a logical step.

You have all heard of transvestites or transsexuals, I am
sure. There are several who have gained international
prominence by undergoing what is euphemistically called
"a change of sex" via surgery and chemotherapy. I do not
condemn any ill person; and I am the first to say that every
adult person has a right to do with his life what he sees
fit, provided he does not endanger the lives of others. If
you want to kill yourself, that's strictly your business; if you
want to commit suicide by a bullet, by LSD, marijuana or
booze—go right ahead. If you want to have your penis
and testicles cut off, that too is your business. You can
live or die any way you wish. But don't tell me and millions
of others that cutting off a penis and de-balling a human
being is "the ultimate adventure"!

That's exactly how the April 8, 1974 issue of *Newsweek*
describes the surgical castration of a British author. Under
the section titled "Ideas" (and by this we assume that surgical transmogrification is seriously to be considered as—
what? The "latest in-thing"?) under the caption "Across the

Frontiers of Sex" (an invitation to youth to fling themselves across "new sexual battlements" leaving genitalia hanging like flags from the barbed wire?), we are given a firsthand glimpse into the wonders of being unmanned. We are told that in the past five years some 600 suffering males have been surgically smoothed-out between the legs; "and in many states Blue Cross will cover the hospital bills."

We are ushered into the inner sanctum of "femaleness" by the latest transmogrified subject who recounts the age-old tale of how he felt more like a "she" since childhood; and now that he's been "briefed" he finds life ever-so-nice and cosy.

Newsweek ecstatically informs its readers (including the scores of sick and suffering emotional castrates who will be sucked into this maelstrom) that the latest "patient" has "come through with flying colors." Praise ye all castrated men! "More important," the obviously entranced *Newsweek* editor pants, the subject "*feels* like the person she always wanted to be." (Note, once your genitals are cut off and your mammary glands are artificially enlarged you are henceforward both surgically [medically] and "legally" *female*.)

Thus, "*he*"—who never had the opportunity or the experience to feel like a "*he*"—now "*feels* like the person she always wanted to be." Of course—if a child cannot be permitted to *feel* like God intended him to feel, if he cannot express his genital love without fear or condemnation, he can become an emotional castrate. Now life is intolerable. Life is not worth living. There is constant sexual pressure. There is continuous, unremitting sexual tension. It can lead to physical illness, as it so often does. It can lead to suicide, as it so often does. No matter how many times he tries "to make it," he can't make it. He's a walking bundle of anxiety, irrational anger, or deep depression.

And what remedy, what relief does society offer? There

is only one answer that irrational armored medicine can offer. Do to the flesh what has already been done to the soul (the emotions).

This barbaric approach will be incomprehensible to the Students of the Future. They will shake their heads in sadness and bewilderment and say, "They were truly madmen in the twentieth century." I must agree. I do not condemn the suffering unfortunates who can find no help in orthodoxy save castration. But I do condemn the *root* of the evil, the condemnation of the Child's Right to Life and Love. And I *do* condemn the mindless *Newsweek* rot that applauds such castration by calling it "a window on the wondrous possibilities of humankind."

> Our Love-Life that cometh from Heaven,
> hallowed be thine existence . . .

OCCULTISM

"Occult" means to hide from sight, to conceal. Occult knowledge is therefore knowledge which is not revealed, which is hidden, secret, mysterious. It pertains to supernatural agencies not detectable by scientific means.

All mystical beliefs contain elements of the occult; and all occult beliefs are deeply mystical. Like political beliefs, occult beliefs range from the extreme right to the extreme left, from the "conservative" belief in angels and demons who are beyond man's understanding and control, to the "radical" occultist beliefs which seek to gain control over supernatural "powers" and enlist them in the service of man.

Mysticism, and thus occultism, is derived from sexual frustration and orgastic impotence. No orgastically potent person would feel the need to engage in the rituals and secrecy of occultism. To join secret cults, to implore the "powers of darkness," to strive to dominate and manipulate people through *power* are all earmarks of Dorized man.

That frustrated and perverse sexuality is the motive power for occultism is abundantly clear in such works as *The Spear of Destiny* by Trevor Ravenscroft (G. P. Putnam's Sons, New York, 1973). The mystic who undergoes psychiatric orgone therapy soon realizes that as the ability to experience pleasurable genital love increases, the irrational need to pursue occult philosophies simultaneously diminishes. Frustrated sexuality is the lure behind the film *The Exorcist*, which broke all box-office records. Armored man is fascinated by acts of depravity, by the grotesque, by the perverse. In the film, a young girl is "possessed" by a demon, masturbates with a crucifix, screams foulest obscenities. Millions paid hard-earned money to see *The Exorcist*, to get their "kicks" from this film; while only a handful will feel attracted to Reich and orgonomy.

Adolph Hitler was deeply steeped in occultism, although raised in a devout Catholic family, as was Stalin. The anti-sexual nature of religions is the breeding ground for occultism. The anti-sexual nature of Communism (although ostensibly the "enemy of religion") likewise breeds an obsession with occultism. Red Fascist scientists are under orders to find answers to the problem of manipulating the masses via occult powers. *The will to power is based upon the inability to love!*

In *The Spear of Destiny*, Ravenscroft makes the connection between Hitler's lust for occult power and his sexual frustrations and perversions:

> Apart from Rauschning, the other leading biographers of Hitler have been unable to perceive that sexual perversion took the central place in (Hitler's) life. . . . They fail altogether to understand that a monstrous sexual perversion was the very core of his whole existence . . . and the motivation behind every act through which he reaped a sadistic vengeance on humanity.

In public, Der Führer would strut and goose-step like a prize cock, spouting his venomous poisons of racial superiority, blood-purity, and the coming destiny of the Germanic "race." In his bedroom, the little moustached house painter would grovel on the floor, begging his current mistress to flog him with a whip. Such was the self-proclaimed "messiah" of the Aryan race! The problem, as Reich pointed out in *The Mass Psychology of Fascism,* is not in the ravings of a psychopathic corporal, but the fact that *millions* of everyday, ordinary, churchgoing, "God-fearing" people yelled "*Sieg Heil!*" and fanatically followed him to destruction and death.

Armored man is fascinated by *power.* He melts like a spinster waiting to be raped when she spies the approaching knight resplendent in shining armor, his sword-penis upthrust at the ready. Hitler had nothing but contempt for the masses. And Stalin was even worse than Hitler, if you reckon in terms of social repression and mass murders.

Christ, the representative of Life and Love on our planet, renounced power as a means of gaining his objectives. He knew that you cannot bring mankind to a knowledge of God by repression and force. He said, "My kingdom is not of this world." Christ knew nothing of the armoring process that turns human beings into mechanized robots and power machines. Christ prayed openly, he wept openly, he ministered to the sick openly, he taught openly. He loved humanity without realizing that the vast majority of his followers were incapable of returning his love with love: they could only hate him. Reich's magnificent work, *The Murder of Christ,* breathes life into an otherwise unreal and mystified Christ.

The followers of Christ, not Christ himself, were mystics. Christ was a virile, healthy genital man. He loved women, and they returned his genital love. And because he was a healthy man, Christ displayed rational anger. He cursed and beat the hell out of the moneylenders in the temple.

He told his followers to "suffer little children to come unto me, for theirs is the Kingdom of Heaven." "*Suffer* little children" means *allow, permit*. He was telling mankind to *allow* children to *know* Love and Life, to permit them genital gratification, not to forbid natural heterosexual expressions.

Christ himself never said "I am God." Nowhere in the words of Christ himself will you find it written that Christ claimed he was God. He said, "The Father is in me and I in the Father." He said, "I can do nothing except it come from my Father." He said, "What I do, you can do also," because the same Love and Life (God) that was in Christ is in Everyman, in every newborn baby.

Christ didn't sit in a dark cellar reciting incantations to malevolent "powers." He didn't smear his face with dog's blood or human blood and demand sexually perverse acts of "allegiance" from his followers. He didn't dress up in expensive robes sewn with silver and gold threads, drink from golden goblets, sleep between the finest linens and then demand poverty, chastity and obedience from his followers. He taught the brotherhood of all mankind under the fatherhood of one God. And he taught mankind to speak simply and directly to their Heavenly Creator. Had Christ appealed to the mysticism and perverse sexuality of the Roman world he would have been crowned King of the World. But precisely because *Christ did not wish power*, his disappointed followers engineered his arrest and deserted him in his final agony—an agony continually experienced by every newborn child in our mechanistic-mystical world.

THE MIASMA OF MYSTICISM

If the natural genital love-life of one generation was affirmed, protected, and permitted gratification, the Kingdom of God on Earth would begin to be a living reality. I said a *living* reality, right here, right now on Earth. And that would herald the end of mysticism and mechanism, and the start of functional, genital man. Therefore the mystics of Earth do not want such a revolution. They want Christ—who is Love and Life—but only as a mirror-image; not as a real, practical, flesh-and-blood way of life.

Sexual frustration and sexual suffering give rise to mysticism, which in turn perpetuates itself by patriarchal, authoritarian sexual suppression. The first thing that missionaries do to primitive peoples is to inculcate a feeling of guilt with regard to natural sexuality. *Mysticism cannot flourish in a healthy sexual environment!*

The magnetism of mysticism is the enchanting *image* of *knowing and feeling* the ever-tantalizing thrill of "Christ," which is one's sexual longings and desires. The masturbatory fantasies of priests, nuns, and "holy" men, and the sexual gratification which they describe in their ecstatic writings clearly reveal the sexual basis of mystical religious experiences. The accent on celibacy, the preoccupation with the confessional (most confessed "sins" are sexual in nature) the "marriage" of nuns to Christ, complete with vows and a wedding band, and the sadistic brutality that exists in schools run by such celibates, all demonstrate the repressed sexual basis responsible for such rituals and authority.

I do not deny the reality of "miracles" in daily life. Life itself is the greatest miracle. I do not deny that many religious mystics perform acts of incredible healing; that the lame walk, the blind see, and the dumb speak. But I attribute all Life, and thus all health and healing, to the divine power that governs our universe: The Life Energy. As our knowledge of God, the Life Energy, increases, such miracles will be known and duplicated according to the functional laws of man and his God.

Granted that an Oral Roberts or a Kathryn Kuhlman can be instrumental in helping a cancer victim or a schizophrenic; yet, they will never touch the *breeding ground* of such pathological conditions, the sexual illness of modern man. And so, for every 10 "cures" ascribed to mysticism, a million more victims will sicken and die because of their inability to experience full pleasure in the genital embrace.

Furthermore, mystical beliefs are often an excuse for not fighting, in a practical manner, the stench and evil which are suffocating our world. Yes, I said mysticism is an excuse for not fighting the evil rot. It is easier to recite litanies than to come to grips with the emotional plague. It is less dangerous to pray to God to "protect my son or daughter," than to actively affirm and socially encourage a healthy love-life for the same son or daughter. And by "easier," I mean it is *cowardice!*

But there can be no salvation without personal work; there can be no "Heaven" without the capacity to give and receive love—*in the body!* All of your prayers and tithings will bring mankind not one inch closer to "the rapture," unless you are prepared to make the word "love" a meaningful reality in the lives of children. Prayers alone will not stop the nuclear pollution and impending death of our globe; prayers alone will not quench the X-rays which are maiming and ruining our infants and children from nuclear reactors, TV sets and fluorescent lights. Prayers alone cannot clean our skies of DOR, the noxious, radioactive Death Energy being poured into our skies by UFOs from Outer Space.°

The only true prayer is Life-Positive work in action!

To be alive *fully* is to experience a daily struggle against the rot in mankind and in yourself that seeks con-

---

°See my book *Planet in Trouble,* Exposition Press, 1973.

stantly to lull you to sleep, to drug you into submission, to tell you that "active opposition to evil is futile and hopeless." Knowledge of Good and Evil without putting such knowledge into practical use in daily life is simply a grotesque illusion and a sham.

The mystics prefers the sham and the illusion. Instead of becoming a pediatrician or a nurse, the mystic will get lost in a monastery or prostrate himself at the feet of some new guru and "meditate" for hours on the "Path of Truth." Instead of stopping the barbarism of circumcision and hospital-nursery-horror-shows in which our newborn babies are daily crucified, the mystics will hide in cathedrals, seek out Tibetan holy men, or bury themselves alive in mountains of mystical tomes *designed to evade the essential.* I understand the attraction for the ascetic life, but I cannot condone it, especially in the young. Happiness is not a static condition of existence. The more one is in contact with Life, the more one is open and sensitive to deep sadness as well as profound happiness. If you cannot find rational ways to Fight for Life, then you are not worthy of Life. And that means, first of all, fighting rationally for your *own* Life, for your own love and happiness.

I never said that living would be easy. I never said that studying Reich and getting involved in orgonomy was a "rose garden"—far from it. If you ever do become deeply involved with orgonomy, there will be times when you will hate me for helping to get you involved, just as there were times when I wished I'd never heard of Reich. You may get very bitter at "evil man"; you will become alienated and very lonely; and you may even be killed for attempting to help humanity to know the reality of Christ as genital love.

But if you prefer your mysticism and your evasion, understand that you are fighting phantoms and shadows reflected in the mirror of your own impotence, and you will never be a true Student of the Future.

ON WORK AND CONTACT

If you can find your way into some type of work *with* Nature, you will have the chance to lead a functional life, and this is quite important. By "functional living" is meant *studying, protecting, and furthering Life,* which, of course, means your own life, first of all. And because the orgone energy is the basis of all life everywhere, in man, Nature, and cosmos, by studying the Life Energy you will be immersing yourselves in functional living.

I have always found it easier to discuss energetic phenomena with farmers, woodsmen, fishermen, children, and young people in general. They are still in touch with life inside and outside themselves. Most so-called "scientists" are not scientists at all; they are at best religious theoreticians or technicians. They study *dead* life, not living, pulsating life. Before Reich, nobody observed living cancer cells under a microscope—everything was killed first, then stained. Incidentally, Reich's *The Cancer Biopathy* has been reprinted by Farrar, Straus & Giroux, the New York publishing company°—you should get a copy, as it is basic to the study of the orgone.

Boring, mechanically repetitive jobs tend to make for mechanical people who must kill the living in themselves in order to continue day after day, year after year, in their mechanized routines. Physicians and nurses who, for the most part, work mechanistically with their patients, become hardened to illness, suffering and death. Modern man has omitted, neglected, and damned the Life Energy in himself and society. He therefore has sacrificed the living for the machine, because we get nothing out of life that is not paid for in some way by our living essence.

°Farrar, Straus & Giroux, 19 Union Square West, New York, N.Y. 10003.

As you travel your various roads in life you will notice that workers who are still in contact with the living—in people and in nature—are more open, generous, sympathetic, and loving. Of course there are exceptions; but you will find that waitresses and cabdrivers are easier to get along with than accountants, lawyers, and bank presidents. Most jobs, for me, became extremely boring and stultifying once they were mastered. I dug ditches for eight hours a day, for some six weeks in Alaska, because I needed the money. I was digging in glacial moraine—a gray soupy mix of gravel and sand, with ice-cold water constantly flowing a few feet beneath the surface. There was nothing to look at but the gray, dirty gravel and the gray dirty cold water, eight hours a day, day after day. I could feel myself contracting with each hour, getting colder and more rigid. I was *becoming* gray and hard and cold, like my work. The worker and his work form a functional unit. Although the pay was good and I needed the money, my body revolted—and finally I threw my shovel out of the ditch, pulled myself out too, and I quit. It was an important experience for me. Now I understood *in my body* what diggers feel, what miners feel, what construction workers feel. I understood what it means to get a paycheck that is just enough to pay your bills and keep you going until the next paycheck, but is not enough to get you out of the hole, literally. I understood how a man can take his paycheck, cash it, and drink his despair away at a bar, while his wife and three children are waiting for him in his dingy, lifeless house. And this condition is a general one all over the planet.

Mankind—which means you and me—will have to find ways to remedy such conditions. Yes, I understand about capital exploiting labor; but do you understand how labor itself exploits labor? Unless you have worked, as I have, with hundreds of men at dozens of jobs, you cannot know how people really feel about work in general, and their own work in particular. Most people work compulsively, because of their character armor. They do the least amount of work required to "get by." This is not the fault of capital nor the fault of labor; *it is the "trap" conditions maintained by armored man—and both capitalists and laborers are armored. If the laborers were tomorrow to become the capitalists, the working conditions would not change one degree, precisely because of the character armor!*

Armored man *is* indifferent, callous, "lazy," unimaginative, greedy and careless. And no workers' revolution in the world has ever changed armored man. Very few workers take real pride in their work. Look how many automobiles have to be recalled each year because of shoddy and careless work. The leftover food on the restaurant dishes of the civilized world, if collected on any one day, could feed millions of starving people. But armored man simply doesn't care. He is concerned about football and baseball scores, or who is running in the Kentucky Derby.

If you ever have built a house or even a small cabin, if you have planted and tended a garden or trees, if you have ever erected a fence, or fixed a toilet or a faucet or rewired a lamp, you have some idea of how exacting and painstaking even the smallest jobs can be. You can take months, or even years, to build a home, then someone can come along and blow it up or burn it down in a matter of minutes. It takes 18, 19, or 21 years to "grow" a soldier who is obliterated in a split second by a bullet, a bomb, or a laser beam. Today, without doubt, The Living appears to be the cheapest commodity in existence.

The Living has not yet learned how to work for Life, to produce solely for Life, to study and comprehend and protect Life. Reich pointed out that there are two kinds of work: vitally necessary work and work which is not vitally necessary. We should affirm and support vitally necessary work, and we should withdraw support (which includes human working power) from the non-necessary work processes. Spending millions to produce food is vitally necessary. But spending *billions* to produce and maintain worldwide armaments is global insanity and global suicide.

Millionaires and billionaires must live with a great deal of guilt concerning their staggering wealth. After all, how many cars can you drive at one time? How many dishes of caviar can you eat at one time? How many suits of clothes can you wear at one time? And no matter what you do, as a millionaire you cannot shut out the face of global starvation and malnutrition and despair.° So once or twice a year you throw a ball to raise money for the Starving Orphans of Krangamania, and this salves your conscience. And your children join radical movements dedicated to "freeing the oppressed" blacks or reds or greens. Your children identify with the oppressed, because of the sexual repression in their own bodies. They identify with prisoners and psychopaths, because they are themselves sick and imprisoned in their muscular armor. So the kids fight irrationally and with desperation, and they too will be ground into the dust by the nameless machine, the Establishment, which is *the nameless and faceless tyrant within their very structures.*

You will have to focus on the essential—on Love, Work, and Knowledge. You will have to focus on *yourself* first. Get yourself straightened out first, otherwise you can only add to the confusion and misery, and we've got more than enough of that already. *All* of our Establishment is not evil! Someone made the dishes you ate from this morning; someone produced the food; someone sewed the clothing you wear; someone picked up the garbage; someone is manning

---

°It is estimated that 5,000 babies die each day on our planet from starvation.

the phone and radio lines you use; someone is at the electric generators, the buses and subway trains; yes, and someone is policing your streets (bravely, conscientiously or inadequately, but his neck is out and vulnerable); and someone is teaching the children of our world; and someone is setting broken legs at your hospital, or unloading ships at thousands of docks, and driving trucks loaded with produce, and manufacturing toilet paper and soap. So don't tell me the Establishment is all bad.

What we have in common is our basic, vitally necessary work, without which none of us could exist for very long—unless you wish to renounce society and live in a hut as a hermit. But I assume you wish to change society *for the better*, and not simply exchange what you have not for what someone else has.

Young people today are in a great turmoil. The moral and social restraints have been loosened and erased too swiftly, and this has left them rootless and without direction. Is it better to have false values than no values? When you are crippled is it better to have a pair of crutches than no crutches? Yes, I'm afraid it is. *And you have no right to remove or ridicule someone's crutches unless you are prepared to get him on his own two feet, walking again!* You just don't go around smashing crutches because they are "evil." Who are you to say that someone else's crutches are "evil." Heal *yourself* first, you would-be physicians of society! Then go out and find a better way to build a better society.

Yet, if you cannot give yourself in love you can only express irrational hatred and anxiety. We hear much about new "liberation armies." How can sick, hateful people build a better world? You don't build a better society by way of machine guns and pistols, by blowing up innocent people, by bombing buildings and robbing banks. But sick, irrational armored man prefers to pose before a mirror with a machine gun in his hands. The gun and the knife and the bomb are substitutes for his impotent genitalia; and that applies to the sexually sick females who join such "liberation" armies. The very road you choose to walk, and the way you walk it, and the companions you walk with—these determine precisely where you will end up.

Every time armored Man was given a choice between Life and Death he has selected the road to Death. Mesmer discovered Animal Magnetism and had caught hold of the Life Energy at precisely the same historic moment that humanity stumbled upon electricity. Man chose electricity. The anesthetic properties of Animal Magnetism conflicted with the chemical discovery of ether. Again mankind had a choice. It chose the chemical anesthetic with all of its attendant post-operative complications. Reich objectified the Life Energy in man and the cosmos at the same historic period that nuclear physicists were playing around with atomic energy—the most powerful destructive force on Earth. Man chose the atom and killed Reich, all but obliterating knowledge of the Life Energy.

Good work takes much time, diligence, patience and love. To do good work you must love what you are doing; but because armored man cannot love at all—either himself, his mate or his work—he can only hate what he is doing, or do it compulsively. He gets his "kicks" out of pursuits that are destructive to his life and to society. Notice the word "kicks." He doesn't feel genuine delightful excitement and a sense of glowing—he gets his "kicks"! To armored man, pleasure is often equated with getting kicked in the ass. It's truly insane—but nonetheless true. When life energy is held in the ass, one feels relief by getting "kicked." One feels a vicarious spark of life in one's genitals by shooting off machine guns, hurting and maiming people, and dynamiting buildings. This is psychopathic behavior, the behavior of the sadist who finds sexual release every time he stabs his victim.

In most people, the Life Energy simply doesn't "sparkle" anymore, as Reich pointed out. We are back again to my analogy of "two kinds of fire"—the glowing flame of the Life Energy or the destructive fire of death. If the Life Energy of a living organism is not capable of luminating in love, then it simply cannot remain static. Orgone energy is never static, never the same, never unchanging. It is always moving—always creating and building, or decaying and dying. You have to understand this and realize it in your body. You have to realize when you are feeling good, when you are able to do good creative work; and you have to know when you feel "out of it," when you have lost contact with yourself, with the orgone energy inside and outside yourself—in brief, when you are *stuck*. And you also must be able to recognize—and this is crucial—when you have a touch of the emotional plague, when you are given to maliciousness in all of its hydra-headed forms: as malicious gossip, as irrational envy or jealousy, as the desire to knock, to condemn, to ridicule, to tell dirty pornographic jokes, *to feel the need to spy*. These things you have to recognize in yourself, so that you can withdraw from any irrational work on the social scene, and clean out the DOR that has collected within you.

Living as functional a life as possible gives you a greater opportunity to remain clean and clear. A person who works with children, trees, animals, nature or plants has a better chance of keeping his Life Energy moving, because he is daily in contact with the living; but you must know the Life Energy underlying the living. If you don't, then you are lost—simply lost, because you will never understand what really *moves* Man and his world, what motivates you, your friends, your countrymen and all Earthmen everywhere—and, what is worse, *you will have no guidelines by which to know whether you are furthering or impeding the Life Energy,* no criterion of judgment, no compass to guide you through personal turmoil, and no lamp to light your way through the darkness of confusion and despair.

THE REICH CASE

I consider the trial of the United States of America *versus* Wilhelm Reich, M.D., the single most important case in man's history. For now, I want to discuss some of the more important highlights of the Reich Case. If you want to study the complete case, I suggest you get a copy of Volume I of *The Journal of Orgonomy* (Box 565, Ansonia Station, New York, N.Y. 10023) and start with the brilliant article, "United States of America *versus* Wilhelm Reich," by David Blasband, A.B., L.I.B.

Reich's discovery of a mass-free, pre-atomic, primordial Life Energy threatened certain powerful commercial and political interests. The gasoline and oil "crisis" showed us just how power rules the world; and power on the political scene is based on power (fuel, food, drugs) on the social scene. And here comes Reich with the discovery of a freely available source of limitless power which was harnessed to run electric motors silently and without pollution. Thus, Reich's discoveries threatened certain commercial hoodlums in and out of government. If Reich's discoveries hadn't been effective, if they really weren't true—that is to say, if they really didn't *work*—he would simply have been dismissed as just another crackpot. We have thousands of crackpots writing on all kinds of nonsensical subjects: How to Make a Million Bucks Overnight; How to Wish Yourself Well; How to Influence Women to Jump Into Bed; How to Cure Cancer and Bedwetting in Ten

Easy Lessons; Fifty Easy Exercises to Regain Sexual Potency, etcetera. You see such works all the time, year after year, and there existence continues.

But here is a Wilhelm Reich—a man with the highest scientific credentials, a brilliant student of Freud, a scientific investigator and thinker of the highest caliber. His books *The Mass Psychology of Fascism, Character Analysis* and *The Function of the Orgasm* are recognized as classics in their field. *Character Analysis,* for example, is a required text in many post-graduate courses for medical students. Anyone with an ounce of God-given sense left in his body knows, after coming to grips with Wilhelm Reich, that here is a serious and brilliant thinker, a researcher who tells you what he did, how he did it, and what his conclusions are. Reading Reich is like touching a high-voltage cable—either you can take it or you cannot; most people cannot.

So what happened? Someone high up in the power structure, someone with tremendous political and financial influence, decided that Reich was too much of a threat to continue working: Reich's work and discoveries constituted a most serious threat to both the power interests of the world (including the food and drug interests) as well as the evil of dictatorships, both of the Red and the Black types (Fascism and Communism).

So a "Complaint" was filed against Reich stating in effect that there is no such thing as orgone energy and that Reich's invention, the Orgone Energy Accumulator, was a fraud. Now, when you study this case, one of the interesting features is the fact that an FDA prosecutor, Peter Mills, had actually been Reich's own attorney for several years. Mills had drawn up many of the papers required by Reich and his research foundation; and Mills had actually notarized papers attesting to the motor force of orgone energy. At the trial, when Mills took the stand, Reich asked him what had induced him "to change sides"—that is, to change from a friend into an enemy. Mills replied that he "had never changed sides." The implication, of course, is that Mills had never been a friend in the first place.

Reich wrote a "Response" to the "Complaint" which he sent to the judge, along with a copy of some 30 years of published material—material containing painstaking laboratory and field experiments, including material written by a score of physicians and scientists who had corroborated Reich's findings and observations.

Instead of studying the material, instead of actually reading Reich's massive scientific and sociological literature, the judge preferred to take the opinion of the FDA prosecutors (all "honorable men") and thereupon signed the Injunction which banned and burned all of Reich's books and published findings and forbade Reich to write another single word about the "non-existent Life Energy." So in August 1956, Reich's books, journals, bulletins, pamphlets, and other scientific literature were dumped into the flaming maw of a New York City incinerator on FDA orders! Included in this "lawful conflagration" were such works as *The Mass Psychology of Fascism, Character Analysis, The Function of The Orgasm,* and *The Murder of Christ*: books which have nothing whatsoever to do with the "therapeutic effects" of the Life Energy. The burning of such literature clearly reveals the *motive* of those who conspired to silence Reich permanently!

Reich's scientific instruments were physically smashed also by FDA order. (Read Peter Reich's *A Book of Dreams*, Harper & Row, New York, 1973.) What faces mankind in the Reich Case are some profound and crucial questions: For openers, let us consider scientific inquiry. What right does anyone, anywhere, have to halt, impede, or quash *new* scientific truth and fact? No one has such a right—and where such power over truth and fact exist you will find a dictatorship. Second—why didn't the judge in the first instance simply read Reich's books, the scientific journals, and the literature sent him *before* he signed the Injunction that halted Reich's research and publications and led inevitably to Reich's death in prison?

Reich stated, again and again, that "laws must be lawful laws, they must not be unlawful laws." He said, "Unlawful laws are automatically null and void." He absolutely refused to obey an *unlawful* law—the Injunction. Many people thought that Reich acted improperly to disobey a court order. But right here is the Gordian Knot that Reich wished to untangle. He made a distinction between a *lawful* and an *unlawful* law. A law that conforms to Truth and Fact is a lawful law—it is *rational*. A law that does not conform to Truth and Fact is an unlawful law—it is *not rational*. Should we obey all laws at all times and under every circumstance, just because a Judge, or a General or a Lieutenant Calley gives them? Do we consider a Nazi concentration camp murderer a "lawful" person because he was simply "following orders" when he executed thousands of people?

Every single judge has a solemn duty and obligation to test the law itself before he applies it in each particular case. Judge John Clifford had an obligation to "do his homework" before he signed the Injunction, because once he signed the Injunction the legal juggernaut was unleashed and nothing could stop it until Reich and his work were smashed to pulp. That was precisely what Reich was trying to prevent.

Let us look at a case closer to home. A neighbor of mine recently divorced his wife, a shrew of a woman who was patently mentally ill. At nearly every full moon, the wife would pack a few things and flee the house with her two children from a previous marriage. She left the husband—my neighbor—thirteen times; and he took her back twelve times. The wife was malicious and vicious. She slandered and ridiculed the husband continually, was insanely jealous, and literally drove the poor man to drink. I watched these events from the sidelines, until at last my neighbor filed, for the third time, for divorce, which was granted.

A few months after the decree of divorce was granted, my neighbor was served with a court order that commanded him to present himself before two physicians to determine his sanity. His ex-wife, still smoldering with hatred and jealousy, had managed to get two doctors to sign a paper which suggested that the man was mentally ill, might be a menace to himself and society, and might require being hospitalized in an insane asylum. By concocting the most heinous fables of sexual depravity and perversity, the ex-wife got a sympathetic judge to countersign the order, which was served by a deputy sheriff upon my friend.

To say the least, my friend was stunned by the court order, which implied that he was insane. He had to hire an attorney. He had to appear before first one physician and then the other, and respond to the assertions made in bitterness and malice by his ex-wife. It was a thoroughly demoralizing experience, a typical example of emotional-plague behavior.

Now—why did the physicians and the judge herself accept, *without question*, the sick and pernicious ravings of the ex-wife? It would have been relatively simple for the judge to make a few phone calls to friends and neighbors, to call in the husband for a private, unofficial chat, and to learn the facts of this situation, facts which would have demonstrated unequivocally that the ex-wife had a history of mental illness, that she at one time had been confined in a mental institution, that she was completely irrational at times, a pathological liar and a menace to her own children. Had the judge done so, the husband would not have had to undergo the kind of emotional-plague harassment that can unnerve the strongest soul. As things worked out, my friend completely vindicated himself, but the incident left strong emotional scars.

Compared to the ordeal of Wilhelm Reich, my friend's tribulations were nothing; however, the same principle applies: Why did not Judge Clifford study the documents, the books, the experimental data, the corroborating articles by many other scientists? Why did he not do so *before he applied the Law?* What happened to Reich and my friend could happen to anyone. If someone doesn't like you, or what you are doing or advocating, he can "get out an injunction" to stop your work, or commit you to an insane asylum; he can tie you up in endless court proceedings which might take months or years and drain you of your financial and human resources. And whether you win or lose you must pay one helluva human price!

"Laws must be lawful to be obeyed." Those involved in the Watergate break-in had a moral obligation to themselves and to Justice to consider whether their impending acts followed "lawful" or "unlawful" orders from the White House. If the President of the United States orders every American citizen to hold his breath for 30 minutes, is such a Presidential decree "lawful" or "unlawful?" Does it conform to Truth? Is it a pro-Life or an anti-Life law?

Is a Court of Law the place to decide scientific questions of the gravest import for mankind? Do conspirators have the right, the legal right, to prohibit research in new fields of scientific inquiry because it will hurt their power status or their pocketbooks? If some new scientific genius discovers how to harness the limitless, *free* cosmic orgone energy to an automobile engine so that it can run effortlessly, without pollution, and without cost—do the oil companies have the unrestrained "right" to manipulate lawyers and judges so that the scientist's inventions are smashed, his protocols burned, and he lands behind bars for "defrauding the public"? That's precisely what happened to Reich, and he was by no means the only scientist who clashed with "Authority," which means the established power structure.

At present, Power & Money rule our world—*power and money*: Not Truth, not Fact, not Justice—*power and money!* Behind every suppressed invention, behind every martyred scientist and thinker, behind every tormented seeker for truth and fact we find the conspiracy of Power and Money —Galileo, Giordano Bruno, Semmelweis, Franz Anton Mesmer, etcetera, etcetera. The history of the advancement of the human race reads like the chapters of a bloody, deadly Crusade to Kill Fact and Truth. And Reich wanted to stop all that murder, once and for all. He came very close. God bless him, he came awfully close.

The Reich Case is your case and my case: It is the trial of good and decent humanity against the Enemies of Man. Read the Reich Case. Study it word for word—especially you would-be scientists and you future attorneys. A magnificent human being fought for Life. Reich's words were penned in his blood and his tears. He wept for Truth, for Justice, for the Children of the Future, for his own children, for himself, and for all Life on the Planet Earth. Reich did not abandon Man—Man abandoned Reich, and thus Man abandoned Life, because Reich was the "*Counsel for the Life Energy, per se.*"

I pass this burning brand to you, the Students of the Future. I have been fighting this fight for some 20 and more years. Make no mistake about it—you who live on Earth: *You are at war!* The Enemy of Man is still in control, and he will destroy you, unless you learn how to recognize him and to fight him effectively. And if you will not Fight for Life, then, frankly, you are not worth Life's effort to keep you alive.

SOME FUNCTIONAL DYNAMICS

The laws of the Life Energy are neither mechanical nor mystical—they are what Reich termed "functional." To understand the orgone both within and outside your body you will have to begin to think *functionally*. But first, you have to know the difference between the living and the non-living—notice, I didn't say the living and the dead, I said the living and the non-living. Reich defined the living organism as *orgone energy pulsating within a membrane*. This pulsation within a membranous structure is specifically what distinguishes the living from the non-living. When the pulsation ceases, "life," as we know it, also ceases.

In pulsation we see two mutually exclusive, but simultaneously identical processes, namely, expansion and contraction. Expansion and contraction of, say, a cell, are two processes which are, at one and the same time, antithetical and mutually exclusive while they are *identical in a common functioning principle* (CFP), which in this case is pulsation. What does this mean? It means that when we are studying a valid energetic process—any process—we have to think in two directions simultaneously, then seek out the common functioning principle which underlies both. As the organism expands in pleasure, the biological orgone moves from the center, the core, to the periphery. It is the movement of the Life Energy that causes the expansion. In contraction, the energy moves toward the core of the organism, causing a simultaneous shift of body fluids from the periphery to the center of the organism. In the former condition we feel "expanded," buoyant and pleasurable; in the latter we feel contracted, cold and anxious.

Anger, for another example, is an expansive expression, the antithesis of anxiety, which is a contractive expression. When you are expressing anger you do not feel anxious;

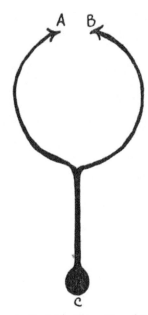

Fig. 1.   Represents Reich's Functional Thought Technique:
A and B are antithetical functions which are simultaneously
identical in a Common functioning Principle, C.

and when you express anxiety you do not feel anger—both,
however, have a CFP in the basic pulsation of your biological orgone energy, which, when unimpeded, expresses
itself as love—immediate and unimpeded pleasurable contact with yourself and your environment.

In the healthy organism, core energy always remains at
a higher potential than peripheral and atmospheric energy.
If this were not so, the energy level of the organism would
be drawn out into the atmosphere and the organism would
cease to live.

So—expansion to the outside and thence back into the
atmosphere; and contraction toward the center, the inside,
the core—expansion and contraction, expansion and contraction, the basic rhythm and pulsebeat of the living, which
in turn moves the fluids, the circulation, gives the impulses

to the heart and all other organs, always expansion and contraction. We take in fresh energy; we use it up and give off the waste products: urine, feces, carbon dioxide, perspiration. The energy is used up in *work*. It is metabolized. Solids are metabolized into solid wastes, liquids into liquid wastes, and orgone into energy waste—DOR! There is also a functional process that converts water into DOR and DOR into water. Reich discovered that in the Arizona desert—I don't want to do anything more here than mention it, however.

But as I ponder some of these energetic processes, a whole bunch of questions comes tumbling into my head. Why, for example, does a blood cell only grow *so* large and no larger? Why does a human being, say, only grow to six feet and not any taller? A tree only 60 feet and not 6,000 feet? What prevents a cloud from covering the sky?

Somewhere in the conceptual process itself, the limitations of form (and hence size) are inherent in the very components needed to "organize" (form) the created bit of living matter or non-living matter. Incidentally, I hope that you will notice that growth and form are two antithetical processes which are simultaneously identical in their common functioning principle, which in this case is what— *creation?*

Energy merging with energy produces matter. Can matter itself merge with energy? Why not? If one element can be transmuted into another element, we must be witnessing an energetic process. Matter itself is frozen energy. It seems perfectly plausible to me that matter itself, conjoined with energy, can grow—does it not indeed do so in the development of an infant into an adult, in a seedling into a full-grown tree? Energy can create or dissipate—it all depends upon the circumstances of the host environment. Energy that goes into the growth of a tree is the same energy that causes the decay and destruction of the same tree. Energy creates matter; and disintegrating matter liberates energy. That's why farmers use manure on their fields. We eat food (matter) which is then broken down into energy. Our bodies are like a living fire—we eat food and drink liquids and metabolize them into energy. We do not "run" on food as such—we run on energy. If you can metabolize the ingested matter you use it as energy; if you cannot, you throw it off as waste, or else it will eventually poison you.

DOR is Life Energy grown stale. Clean, flowing water doesn't grow stale. Stagnant water grows stale, and stale water gives rise to putrefaction, decay, the formation of microorganisms which arise from the decay, which feed off the decay and which further contribute to the decay process.

DOR is also Life Energy which has been used up. I suspect that there are many DOR variants, or DOR-carriers, wherein the concentrations of DOR determine their life-negative qualities, from carbon, carbon monoxide, to nuclear radiation. A certain amount of carbon, for example, is essential for living Life—too much is deadly. We are back again to the "razor's edge of existence" to which the living process is confined on our planet. Too much or too little is always the problem in order to maintain healthy life, healthy functioning.

Remember, too, that what we quantify as clicks on a Geiger counter or as peaks on a graph is simply the atmospheric Life Energy or the biological Life Energy *reacting* to an extremely irritating, life-negative source. Goldfish can exist peaceably and healthily in a pond of water; but if you disrupt that water with a high-powered outboard motor, if you churn up the water continuously with powerful propellers, the fish will die—*not* from the high-powered propeller blades, per se, but from the reaction of the propellers *upon the water!* The water, of course, is the atmospheric Life Energy for fish.

Nuclear physicists, ignorant of the atmospheric Life

Energy, cannot understand what their poisonous nuclear energy—even in "minimal, safe amounts"—is really doing to our planetary Life-Energy medium, how it creates oranur.

We always go back to the problem of how to maintain a healthy energy economy, in the atmosphere or the living organism. Armored man has for hundreds of years been creating more DOR than he can adequately handle. He consistently causes desert development by disrupting the peaceful energetic processes in his offspring and his environment. He actually makes deserts—as Reich showed—of his children and of his planet. Desert man can only reproduce deserts, both inside and outside himself. If you don't believe this, ride in the smoking car of any train or ferry—the polluted atmosphere will choke any healthy person to death. Look at how trees are cut down indiscriminately, how the land is "clear-cut" (scalped would be a better word) how dustbowls develop from overuse and greed.

Recent infrared photographs taken from aircraft flying over New York City indicate a great increase of "heat" arising from that city, and very likely *all* cities. Why?

Cities are breeding grounds for oranur and DOR. They consist of millions of accumulators, alternating layers of concrete or plaster and steel, plus God only knows how many fluorescent lights, nuclear sources, X-ray machines, millions of TV sets, high-voltage electricity, neon lights, carbon monoxide from auto exhausts, rubbish burning, garbage smoldering, and the people themselves—DORized and dazed and dying. And then there are the burgeoning nuclear plants, with their boiling, deadly waste-products, their radioactive fumes. And what about the thousands of miles of tarred pavement and reinforced-concrete sidewalks. In farm and tree country, the atmospheric OR undulates and penetrates and interacts easily and "peacefully" with the natural landscape. But in a city, the OR is confined, "confused" and battered by the numberless irritants. It has to *force* its way through thousands of miles of tarred roadway and millions of walls of steel and concrete. Everywhere the orgone is constantly being irritated, goaded, stimulated, strained, forced, and driven to a frenzy of activity—i.e., *oranur!*

But that's precisely what armored man desires, is attracted to, thrives on, and perpetuates. He cuts down his trees and wild flowers, and manufactures plastic, dead "plants and flowers" to decorate his homes and offices. And it all starts with the human animal, the infant, the Christ-child born into a world of insanity. Armored man prohibits a healthy genital development, prohibits a healthy heterosexual development, then goes out and buys huge inflated, plastic dolls to sleep with as a substitute for healthy heterosexual human love. And this, too, we have to understand.

I see that I have raised more questions than I have answered. But the basic thread running through all of this is the function of the Life Energy in man and his world, how and why we got off the track of healthy living, and what we must concentrate on in order to survive and build a better world.

THE MARRIED CONDITION

Compulsive marriage has been falling apart rapidly in the twentieth century. Nothing is the subject of more gossip than peoples' marital condition: Who is sleeping with whom today? Armored man wants "freedom" but when he comes face to face with it, it disturbs the hell out of him. He wants the freedom to screw around for a weekend, then demands more stringent divorce laws.

You live with your mate in a condition of mutuality either out of a rational or an irrational need. You enter into a marriage when you find a mate who gives you the genital gratification you require—that's basic, assuming, of course, you have the capacity for a healthy love-life. Nobody has to say formal prayers over you to "marry" two people. Who "marries" the birds? Who married the pioneers who lived isolated, far from any city, from any church or preacher?

The anxiety of armored man requires him—compels him—to be rubber-stamped, "officially married." Yes, I realize there are others factors, social and legal. But some states still recognize common-law marriages, which automatically apply when two people live together for a certain number of years.

A good marriage is the greatest asset for any person. The mates grow and develop together. Setbacks and troubles mutually experienced have a way of deepening life together. Your mate is not only your lover and companion, but also your most trusted friend. But you have to pay a price for anything—and so it is with marriage.

Whatever you do, don't have children right away—at least not the first year, and perhaps not until the second or third year. If the marriage doesn't work out, you're simply stuck, and you've brought a great responsibility into the world. And a baby born into an unsettled and unsettling atmosphere can only suffer from it. God knows we've got enough unwanted and "burdensome" babies—millions of them. If your love-life is unsatisfactory, you'll take out your frustration and anger on the innocent baby, you'll be contributing to another Murder of Christ.

You should have a child because you want it and are ready for it—emotionally and financially, and not because it was an *accident!*

Furthermore, you're going to have to be strong enough to fight the emotional plague, in society and in yourself, which will seek to crush the life in your infant and child. And you will need to grow deep roots in your mutual love-life with your mate before you can adequately handle the emotional plague.

I said you have to pay for everything you receive in this life—that includes the love from your mate, and it includes having children. The old, wise saying is very true: "You cannot have your cake and eat it, too." As you live and love together you will notice that familiarity breeds boredom. Nothing can remain the same—not even your first passionate embraces; everything changes, it grows or decays. The twentieth century is not set up for self-regulated marriage. This is a whole new and different ball-game, and it will require deep changes in society before self-regulated marriages can develop and continue functionally.

What we are witnessing in the last part of the twentieth century is armored man fucking around without restraints. We are witnessing socially accepted pornography and licentiousness—but don't mistake these for self-regulated behavior on the part of genital human beings.

If you have a happy, satisfying love-life, everything else will be easier; if not, everything else will seem "impossible." Somebody has to make the meals and wash the dishes and take out the garbage and diaper the baby; and these chores continue for months and years. The husband says he is involved in "functional work," he's a scientist or a writer, "too far above" such everyday, mundane pursuits. Or the wife is an editor or an artist, and she, also, is "too far above" such mundane pursuits. Having money, being able to hire help—these can aid the situation. But the old battle between freedom and responsibility must continually be settled. And when *your* baby arrives, your first and foremost responsibility is always to the infant: that goes for the husband as well as the wife. That's why I emphasize that the baby must *not* be an "accident," because if it is, then your resentment will be greatly magnified.

And whether or not you have a child is ultimately the wife's decision: It's her body, her sustenance, her emotional structure that are involved in the growth and initial development of the baby. As long as the foetus is physically and bio-energetically dependent upon the mother's organism, only the mother should have the final word as to whether or not she wants that baby. This is not the business of any Church, social organization, or anti-abortion fanatics—*it is strictly the mother's concern!*

Don't think for one minute that *your* marriage is going to be a "happy-ending" Hollywood romance for the rest of your life. It won't. You can't stay in bed 24 hours a day. You'll get hungry, bored, and will need work to do—believe it or not. Both mates should be as independent in their work as they are dependent in their affection and love; and both partners should encourage each other along the lines of independency, of independent growth in whatever interests each person. The so-called artistic pursuits are no more important than the physical jobs required by society. How would the artist survive if the farmer did not produce? No particular kind of life-positive work is intrinsically better than any other, be it work with the mind or the body. Man requires more than food, clothing, shelter and a mate to enjoy life, and so music, dance, art, writing, also contribute and should be fostered. There are only two kinds of "work": Life-positive, vitally necessary work, and "work" which is actually *non-work*—that is, it is not vitally necessary to human life and society in general. Today, politics and war-manufacture are totally *anti-life*.

But I have strayed from our considerations of marriage. It takes a long time to really learn to know someone, to learn to love deeply, to adjust, to give as well as take, to accommodate each other. Usually one partner is dominant and will strive to "change" the other. Both should be able to get out any resentment, to speak out when they feel hurt or slighted or disadvantaged. This is essential in keeping a marriage alive. The partner who holds the purse strings automatically has an advantage—that's why both should be as independent as possible. A good "hair-down," tooth and claw fight (I don't mean physical abuse) will clear the air very rapidly, and making up afterwards is very sweet indeed.

If you want your mate to succumb to cancer, make her feel useless, anxious, guilty, worthless and absolutely dependent upon your every will and whim! That goes for the women as well. But, of course, *you* won't do that—will you?

And you, young woman, if you want your husband to shrivel up and die long before his time, tie a rope around his neck and pen him up at home—don't give him the freedom to follow his own pursuits and inclinations, nag the hell out of him, question his every move, and when his every venture goes down the drain, remind him continually that "you told him so."

There are no rules for a successful marriage—nothing absolute. Everyone is different, each marriage is different and unique. And, besides, a "successful" marriage cannot be based on the number of years you stay together. A successful marriage may last a year or less—or twenty-five, or for life. Who is to say, except the parties involved? The criterion is the amount of pleasure living with one's mate affords. And if you have the capacity for deep love, you have also the capacity for deep sorrow, for growth and development, and for *rational* anger.

No one knows what form will be taken by marriage of mates in the future, but it is certain that the role of the family, its structure, its attitude toward healthy genitality in children—all of these will play a crucial role in future societies. People who have the capacity for healthy genital love will not tolerate any compulsion in morality or in marriage. Children will be carefully planned for, tenderly loved. Self-regulation and love will replace the compulsive straight-jackets that pass today for "happy" marriage. Remember always that the only way to enjoy life and love is with an open hand. If you've ever had the privilege of holding a bird in your hand you will understand what I mean: The more you close your fingers, the more anxious the bird becomes to fly from you.

Part Two
What Is God's Word?

INTRODUCTION

Is there a God? And if so, how can we know the *truth* regarding God's word? These two questions have haunted me since my earliest youth, when I was strongly attracted to the words of love and wisdom spoken by Jesus Christ as recorded in *The New Testament*.

In my book *Orgone Energy—The Answer to Atomic Suicide*, I presented one chapter devoted to this subject, "Toward the Discovery of God." This single chapter, represented by only a few pages, took a year of thought, writing and rewriting. It was the most difficult piece of writing I had ever undertaken. I was deeply moved by the implications and magnitude of Reich's discoveries as they pertained to "God." And I realized while writing the chapter, that the subject itself was too vast, and my year of effort scarcely scratched the surface.

Now I would like to approach the subject from a different direction, and it is fitting that we begin on Easter Sunday, 1974, when millions are celebrating the resurrection of Christ—that is, the belief that death brings rebirth, and that the grave is not the final disposition of life. It is ironic that on this day, as recorded in the *Spokesman-Review* (Spokane, Wash.), another nuclear-radiation leak has been reported at the Hanford, Wash., nuclear-reactor plant. The Life Energy and Death Energy continue to vie for supremacy over our planet, just as the principles of Christ and the emotional plague continue their relentless struggle for Man's emotional life.

The Holy Bible has been a very dear friend of mine for many years. From it I have gained strength and great comfort during many trying times.

To my mind the Bible is the single greatest literary work ever published. Reading it, I feel deep contact with

people of bygone ages, their struggles, their hopes, their
fears and frustrations, their search for truth, and their endless quest for God. Moreover, the prose and poetry of the
Bible are unsurpassed in the English language, and the social structure of modern society has deep and abiding roots
in biblical writings and wisdom.

As you know, one of my greatest pleasures is to converse
with people on matters close to my heart, to bounce our
thoughts off each other in a sympathetic and friendly
examination of fact and truth. It has been my experience,
however, that such a friendly exchange of opinion and verbal exploration are impossible when one is talking with a
religious fanatic. And by a religious fanatic I mean anyone
who holds an unquestioning, *static* view of life, morality,
science, history, "destiny", economics, or the nature of man.

Our universe is predicated upon the existence of an *ever-
changing, moving, and continuously creating Life Energy*.
It is this Life Energy that changes our todays into our
tomorrows. Thus nothing, *nothing* will be tomorrow as it
is today: not you, not me, not the sky, a tree, a mountain,
the "truth" or our most cherished beliefs. What I am writing
at this very instant, I could not write in the exact same way
tomorrow, because tomorrow I will be a different person;
and a year from now an even more different person. I will
grow or I will decay. But I can never be a static entity.

Armored man prefers the static and the absolute, simply
because he cannot tolerate the change which contact with
the orgone requires. As Mesmer stated, "life moves from a
state of fluidity to one of solidity." When we are young we
seek change, we desire change, and we openly and actively
participate in trying to change society—hopefully for the
better. As we grow older, more armored, more rigid (more
"solidified") we become conservative in our attitude toward
life, toward society, and toward change itself.

The religious fanatic has both feet mired in the static-
absolute. He unquestioningly accepts as dogma certain basic

tenets, be they "religious" or "socio-economic." The fanatical Communist never questions the basic tenets of Communism—they are pure, inviolate, and immutable, therefore dogma. Dogmatic beliefs are functionally identical with one's character armor. The muscular armoring process is the physical counterpart of the indoctrination process. To question dogma is to threaten the character armor. This is especially true in the field of science. And so when you discuss energetic processes with a religious fanatic you are in fact threatening his very armored existence. He must oppose your threat; he must fight you, with words and arguments, with malice and guile, or—if you stir him up too much—with threats and violence.

To the fanatical religionist, The Bible is the static-absolute, unchanging, not-to-be-questioned *word* of God.

Now—you and I, together, will attempt to uncover, with fresh eyes, whether the Bible is, in fact, the unquestionable, truthful, factual, rational and logical "revealed word of God" as presented to man by so-called prophets and holy men. For hundreds of years, religious leaders and preachers have told humanity that the Bible is strictly factual, literally truthful, absolutely consistent, lacking contradiction and falsehood. I propose that we should examine such allegations of truth, fact, and consistency by referring to one basic source: The King James version of the Bible, containing both the Old and the New Testament.

To aid us in our inquiry, we solicit the services of a brilliant bible scholar and jurist, the late Major Joseph Wheless, formerly judge advocate of the U.S.A., associate editor of the *American Bar Association Journal*, member of the American Law Institute, and a lifelong student of the Bible. Major Joseph Wheless' book *Is It God's Word?* (Alfred A. Knopf, New York, 1926) is a veritable biblical blockbuster. Perhaps some day it will be republished in its entire 506 pages. It is, to my mind, the most illuminating critical examination of the Bible ever written, and I wish to acknowledge my total indebtedness to Major Wheless, whose patient dedication to truth and fact should not go unrecorded .

So, with *The Bible* on the one hand, and Major Wheless acting as Judge Advocate of Truth and Fact, let us begin our quest into "the word of God."

In his introductory remarks, Wheless makes an extremely important observation which we should consider:

> If we find that the "Word of God" tells the same story in two or more totally different and contradictory ways, or that one inspired writer is "moved by the Holy Ghost" of Yahveh to tell his tale one way, and another inspired writer is moved to tell it in another way, totally different and contradictory in the essence of the alleged facts of the same event, we are forced to know and confess that one or the other record at least is wanting in God's inspiration of truth and is inevitably false. This being so, and there being no possible way of determining which version is the false and which may not be, both must be rejected as equally false, or equally uninspired and incredible; and in either event, the theory of inerrant inspiration and of the revealed truth of the "Word of God" is irreparably destroyed. (p. 49)

Now Wheless proceeds to examine the testimony of truth, as given in the Bible itself, from "Genesis" to "Revelation." The examination is devastating. As Wheless points out, the very name "Adam" is simply a deception created by the translators of "Genesis." In the original Hebrew language, the text in which the Bible was written, the word "Adam" never appears as a proper name, as there are no capital letters in the Hebrew script. The Hebrew word, mistranslated as "Adam," simply is "ha-adam," which means *the-man,* and is a common noun.

The very first instance of the mention of man, *adam,* occurs in Genesis 1:26—"And Elohim (gods) said, Let *us* make man (*adam*) in *our* image"; "and Elohim created *ha-adam* (the man) in his image" (1:27).

In Genesis 2:7, "Yahveh formed *ha-adam* (the-man) out of the dust of *ha-adamah* (the ground)." And so, as Wheless correctly points out, there was never an "Adam", capitalized as a proper noun, since the word itself refers to the species "man" throughout the Hebrew scriptures. In Hebrew, man is referred to as *"adam"* simply because he was formed out of *adamah,* the earth, or ground! the word *homo* (man) is derived from the word *humus,* the ground. Wheless further notes that the prophet Ezekiel repeatedly refers to Yahveh (God) as addressing him as *"ben-adam"*— that is, son of man, which is precisely the expression used many times by Jesus when referring to himself.

Thus there never was an "Adam" as such, but simply a species, *adam,* man, *referring to all of humanity.* And without an "Adam," named as such, the doctrine of original sin based on the transgressions of an individual "Adam" becomes thoroughly untenable.

NOAH'S ARK

The famous flood in the days of Noah presents us with problems of animal census. In Genesis 6:19, God commanded Noah "of *every* living thing of all flesh *two of every sort* shalt thou bring into the Ark, to keep them alive with thee; and they shall be male and female." And, later, in 6:22, we are assured that Noah did precisely what God commanded, taking *two of every kind* into the ark. But in the very next chapter (7:2) God's order to Noah reads, "Of every clean beast thou shalt take to thee by sevens, the male and his female; and of the beasts that are not clean by two, the male and his female." This latter dictum is again contravened in 7:8,9—"Of clean beasts, and of beasts that are not clean, and of fowls, and of every thing that creepeth upon the earth, there went in *two and two* unto Noah into the ark, the male and the female . . ."

At this point, too, the ability of Noah to discriminate

between "clean' 'and "unclean" beasts is itself quite puzzling, inasmuch as the concept of exactly *what* was either "clean" or "unclean" was entirely unknown on earth until the law of kosher (cleanliness) was allegedly given by Moses about 1,000 years later (Leviticus 11). How, asks Judge Advocate Wheless, could Noah possibly know the difference?

FURTHER CONFUSIONS AND CONTRADICTIONS

Reading Wheless is a shattering, eye-opening experience. Truth is indeed "a terrible, swift sword," and it is understandable that ministers, preachers, and religious fanatics shun Judge Advocate Wheless' iconoclastic truths as too intolerable. When one lives all his life in the darkness of "blind faith" and unchallenged dogma, the light of truth, indeed, cannot be suffered. Nevertheless, as Students of the Future, we are committed to Truth and Fact, regardless of whose pet theories are jeopardized, whose chairs of learning are overturned, or whose vested interests are endangered. And so let us continue.

In Genesis 10 and 11, we are told the story of the building of the Tower of Babel, and the subsequent edict of God which resulted in the "confusion of tongues." Genesis 10 describes the families and descendants of the sons of Noah, Shem, Ham and Japhet, detailing how, in a period of some 144 years since the Flood, the descendants had proliferated into many separate nations. These separate nations (about 20 are named) lived in great cities and "were divided in their lands, every one after his tongue" (Genesis 10:5). This would certainly appear to indicate that there were *many* separate nations, "divided in their lands," each nation speaking a separate language "after his tongue." The specific phrase noting the differences in language ("after his

tongue") is emphasized twice more (Genesis 10:20,31)—
for a total of three times. Thus there can be little doubt that
all of these disparate nations, extending from Assyria to
Gaza, were in fact speaking different languages.

Yet, the very first verse of the eleventh chapter of
Genesis proceeds to tell us: "And the whole earth was of
one language, and of one speech."

Then all of these diverse nations, formerly "divided in
their lands," and "every one after his tongue," suddenly
agreeably decide to journey together until they "found a
plain in the land of Shinar," where again, suddenly and
agreeably, they decided to build a new city and a tower
"whose top may reach into heaven."

Thereupon, we are informed, Yahveh heard of this am-
bitious undertaking and he "came down to see the city
and the tower" (Gen. 11:5). And the Lord spoke (presumably to someone) and said, "Behold the people is one,
and they have all one language . . . Go to, let *us* go down,
and there confound their language, that they may not
understand one another's speech" (Gen. 11:6,7). And
Yahveh "scattered them abroad from thence upon the face
of the earth" (Gen. 11:8). Following this ungodly confusion and turmoil, the Bible informs us that because God
"did there confound the language of all the earth" the
place was named "Babel." And here Wheless makes another
pointed comment:

> It may be wondered which of them [that is, the divided
> nations now speaking in languages totally incomprehensible to
> each other] called it Bab-el, for all their languages now at least
> were different, and what would be Babel in one of them might
> be a foreign word meaning the Bowery, or Hoboken, or Hell in
> some of the others.

One additional point before we leave our Tower of
Confusion, supposedly aptly named "Babel." The English
word "babel," taken from biblical history, means "a confusion of voices," or "a place of such confusion." In the

Hebrew tongue, the word *Bab-el* simply means "Gate of God," just as *Beth-el* means "house of God." And to further confuse the confusion, Genesis 10:10 informs us that Nimrod had already built a city called "Babel." So what was Babel (Gate of God) in Genesis 10:10, was by some linguistic legerdemain transformed into Babel (a city of confusion) in Genesis 11:9.

Let us pause here momentarily and consider these things from the long viewpoint of mankind and man's history. What disturbs me most about these "inviolate" and "unquestionable" biblical truths is the *tenacity*, the unthinking blind and dogmatic tenacity with which men, for hundreds of years, have accepted (and I include my youthful self here) such "God-given facts"!

The same rigid character structure which cut man off from seeing and knowing the Life Energy in himself and Nature—this same rigid muscular armoring prevents armored man from asking basic questions, from knowing fact from falsehood, from *touching truth*. Orgone energy has always existed in man and his universe; yet, for thousands of years mankind could not make contact with it. And where truth cannot prevail, then the counter-truth must prevail. When man lost touch with his true God, *as the Love and Life Energy which is the foundation of all existence*, then he was forced to invent and to conform to fable, myth and dogma.

Without a deep knowledge of the Life Energy (God) man plunged headlong into Hell. Therefore we cannot and must not criticize any blindly accepted dogma with contempt and superciliousness. We must always strive to handle the sick body politic with sympathy and understanding. One has no right to *force* truth upon those who cannot tolerate it, or to *force* truth as "Truth" to be itself blindly accepted. At the same time, however, the Student of the Future demands that fable, falsehood and dogma must themselves never be forced upon anybody, especially the

young. In a clean, honest and open contest between Truth
and Falsehood, the Truth is strong enough to stand on its
own, and this is particularly true of *New Truths*. Like new
wine, new truth cannot be placed in old bottles. New truth
requires new vessels, mobile character structures, otherwise the new truth cannot be contained—it will become
soured, perverted, and will end up flowing into the very
sewers you will be attempting to clean up, adding to the
mess.

With this in mind, let us return to our considerations of
The Bible, a work that represents the best as well as the
worst in the confused and aspiring creature we recognize
in each other.

CONTINUING CONUNDRUMS

If the Bible is—as religious fanatics claim—the "inspired, unimpeachable and wholly consistent Word of God,"
revealed to duly constituted prophets and soothsayers
(truth-sayers), then we should expect the given "word" to
withstand close scrutiny in this regard. However, as we
diligently search the scriptures for the factual truths
allegedly contained herein, our faithful trust continues to be
shaken. Examples follow.

Moses is told by God, "Thou canst not see my face,
for there shall no man see me and live" (Exodus 33:20).
But the author of this passage evidently forgot that Moses
had already seen God's face: "And God spake unto Moses
face to face" (Exod. 33:11), and Moses nevertheless remained alive.

Everyone knows the story of David's match with Goliath;
how the youthful David, carrying only a sling and a few
pebbles, loaded his sling and smote the giant with one

shot in the forehead (1 Sam. 17:49). Yet the entire tale stretches credulity beyond repair when we read, about 40 years after this heroic event, that when David was king and warring against the Philistines, there was "a battle in Gob with the Philistines, where Elhanan the son of Ja-areoregim, a Bethlehemite, slew Goliath, the Gittite, the staff of whose spear was like a weaver's beam" (2 Sam. 21:19). Now the translators of this passage, apparently realizing that a Goliath once dead could not be slain twice, perpetrated a "faithful fabrication" by inserting into the text the words "slew *the brother* of Goliath." Since the words *the brother* are italicized to show that they do not appear in the original text, one has good reason to consider the entire tale as suspect. (The *New American Standard Bible*, Creation House Inc., Carol Stream, Ill., 1971, omits the words "the brother" entirely.)

Even the death of King Saul is not related without contradiction. In 1 Samuel 31:4, after the armour-bearer of the defeated Saul refused to kill him (as Saul had ordered), Saul committed suicide: "Saul took a sword and fell upon it" (31:4) and died (31:5). But in 2 Samuel, the story is otherwise. Saul asked a young Amalekite who was on the scene "by chance" (2 Sam. 1:6)—and thus could not have been the king's armour-bearer—to kill him. And this passer-by complied with Saul's wishes and killed Saul (2 Sam. 1:10).

PARADOX OF THE PLAGUES

Famous in biblical folklore is the terrible destruction wrought by God via his principal agent Moses upon the stubborn Egyptian king who would not grant free passage to the enslaved Hebrews.

Advocate of Truth, Joseph Wheless, turns his piercing critical gaze on these "miraculous plagues" and the results

are as devastating to "biblical verities" as the plagues themselves were to all of Egypt.

We shall pass over the several minor plagues performed
by Moses and his divine rod, and focus on the contest between God and the Pharaoh of Egypt, wherein God sent
a "very grievous murrain [pestilence]" on the Egyptian
cattle of every kind, "and all the cattle of Egypt died"
(Exod. 9:3-6). Yes, it states categorically "all the cattle
of Egypt died." Not just some, or certain types of cattle,
but "all the cattle of Egypt," which means cows, oxen,
sheep, camels, asses and horses. All dead!

And before the carcasses of presumably thousands, if
not tens of thousands, of the dead cattle had time to rot,
the Lord Yahveh sends yet another plague of boils and
blains "upon man and upon beast" (Exod. 9:10,11),
although which beasts were still alive to suffer this additional plague remains incomprehensible, since they were
all dead!

Not content to kill all Egyptian cattle by the "grievous
murrain," followed by the "boils and blains," the unimpeachable biblical testimony records that on the next day
Moses announced that a "grievous hail" (Exod. 9:18)
would kill every man and every beast that remained in
the open fields. And the hail came as predicted and killed
every man and beast (Exod. 9:24,25). Thus the same cattle
first totally destroyed by the "grievous murrain," succumbed
to the "boils and blains" and suffered yet a third time to be
killed again by the "grievous hail."

GOD AS SUPERMAN

In searching the ancient Hebraic scriptures of *The Old
Testament* with eyes stung open by the prestigious genius
of Joseph Wheless, we are compelled to conclude that God

(Yahveh) of the *Old Testament* is nothing less than Man's primitive need for and conception of a Superman.

From the very beginning of the Bible, God is presented in humanlike form, with anthropomorphic qualities. Scriptural writers and "authorities" made the grievous mistake of projecting human, armored qualities from man to "God," instead of attempting to study God's Natural Law which is the only true path to knowing God. Not until the work of Wilhelm Reich, however, was this pathway opened. Let us study some of the "attributes of God" as projected and fantasized by armored man.

That God is manlike is readily apparent in Genesis: "God created man in his own image, in the image of God created he him." And, further, "male and female created him them" (Gen. 1:27,28). The implication is that God represents *both* the male and the female principle, which is of course factually correct, since sexuality as such is derived from the Godhead of the cosmic orgone energy ocean. Hence "God" cannot be either "male" or "female," but must be the common functioning principle of both sexes—patriarchal, sex-negating scripture notwithstanding.

This primitively conceived "God" came down to earth, walked about, and even made clothing of skins for Adam and Eve. Again, as a man, he came down to watch the construction of the Tower of Babel (Gen. 11:5). He stood on the rock at Horeb and watched Moses smite it for water (Exod. 17:6). He came down again as an angel and engaged in a wrestling match with Jacob, and Jacob testified "I have seen God face to face" (Gen. 32:30); although previously, as we have noted, this God-man had said, "Thou canst not see my face; for there shall no man see me and live."

John contradicts the possibility of such a confrontation between God and Moses or God and Jacob in the flat assertion, "No man hath seen God at any time" (John 1:18). And this contradiction is itself contradicted when St. John the Divine reveals that he saw both God and his Son sitting side by side on the throne of glory (Rev. 3:21), describing God's hair, eyes, and feet.

Thus God as Superman, with human passions, jealousies, and anger—as well as human sexuality—is presented to us throughout these ancient scriptures. It is this God-man who fought with drawn sword at the battle of Jericho (Josh. 5:13). He is called "mighty and terrible" (Deut. 10:17), a characterization repeatedly reiterated, by Isaiah, by David, by Jeremiah, and others.

And this Superman-God is not above killing without reason—as after the first meeting between Moses and God at the burning bush. Here God first orders Moses back to Egypt and then waylays him behind an inn and seeks "to kill him" (Exod. 4:24), thus making God an assassin.

Besides raining down plagues on helpless and innocent men, women and children (not to mention cattle) this Superman-God is credited with deliberately destroying *all mankind* in the Flood. And to His own elected Chosen People he is depicted as no less atrocious. He is constantly being provoked into anger, burning the Hebrews (Num. 11:1); smiting the Chosen Ones with plague (Num. 11:33); sending deadly serpents to bite them (Num. 21:5,6); and slaying *twenty-four thousand* of them for lusting after Moabite maidens (Num. 25:9).

Because Uzzah attempted to prevent the Sacred Ark from falling off the oxcart, this "merciful" God killed him. Because others dared to look into the Ark, more than *fifty thousand* additional Hebrews were slaughtered by this Superhuman (1 Sam. 6:19). And even this wholesale butchery was exceeded by the same deity who murdered *seventy thousand* of "His Chosen" in one day (2 Sam. 24:15).

And our biblical *Old Testament* "God" is quite capable of lying: The first recorded lie being the threat made to Adam: "In the day that thou eatest therefrom thou shalt surely die" (Gen. 2:17). Adam ate the fruit and nonetheless survived to age 930! This same "law-giving God" directed Moses to lie to the Pharaoh (Exod. 3:18). And Ezekiel fully acknowledges the lying propensities of "God" by imputing all prophetic lies as being instigated by God Himself: "If the prophet be deceived . . . I Yahveh have deceived that prophet" (Ezek. 14:9). Abraham found it necessary to remind his deity: "Shall not the Judge of all the earth do right?" (Gen. 18:25).

On and on throughout the Scriptures, characterologically armored man projects upon "God" the qualities and attributes of armored man himself. Armored man lies, deceives, is irrationally angry, kills out of his armored anger or anxiety, commits countless atrocities, and then projects all of these sick and distorted characterizations upon his "God." It could not be otherwise. If a man is sick and cut off from Nature and himself, he can only project such sickness upon others. He justifies his evil by claiming it is "divinely inspired." He hears and feels *forces* (*à la* Hitler) compelling him to victimize the weak and helpless. Armored man conceives of "God" as a merciless, pitiless, arrogant and atrocious Superman. Only a Genital Man, such as a Christ or a Wilhelm Reich, in full contact with Nature and with God as Love and Life, could conceive of "God" as creative, life-giving, life-affirmative, "merciful," compassionate and "long-suffering"—the Life Energy of Man and his Universe.

GOD THE FATHER

It has been diligently and consistently proclaimed by exponents of Christianity that Jesus Christ was the "only begotten Son of God," although Christ himself said he was "the son of man." In truth, *all* children are sons or daughters of God, inasmuch as we are creations of the Life Energy.

To show that God never sired but *one* earthly child, as the misinterpreters of the Bible would have us believe, Wheless offers the following incontrovertible examples of "God's" paternalistic proclivities:

God had made a promise to Abraham that his wife Sarah would bear a son. Sarah laughed when she heard this news, and said to God: "After I am waxed old shall I have pleasure, my lord being old also?" God responded: "Is anything too hard for God?" (Gen. 18:12, 14). Now when Sarah referred to herself as being too old for pleasure, "my lord being old also," she meant that both she and her husband had passed the point in life when sexual intercourse was a mutually pleasurable experience. In short, neither husband nor wife had the excess biological energy for genital pleasure. Implicit also in Sarah's statement was the biological fact that she considered herself beyond the age of child-bearing.

So what happened? "And God visited Sarah as he had said, and God did unto Sarah as he had spoken. For Sarah conceived and bare Abraham a son" (Gen. 21:1,2). Abraham never "begat" the son conceived "by God" and delivered of Sarah.

Again we find another "barren" wife, this time the wife of Manoah. She too was visited by God "as she sat in the field: but Manoah her husband was not with her." And God told this woman: "Behold, thou shalt conceive, and bear a son"; and in the natural course of such events, "the woman bare a son, and called his name Samson" (Judges 12:7,9,24).

Yet another case of deistic paternity is recorded, with the fruit of this union resulting in quintuplets: "And God visited Hannah, so that she conceived, and bare three sons and two daughters" (1 Sam. 2:21). And, of course, there is the birth of Jesus, after the "Virgin Wife" of Joseph conceived, and the disturbed Joseph reportedly learned from God himself that He was father to the child: "Thou art my son; this day have I begotten thee" (Heb. 1:5; 5:5).

Which brings up the interesting question of the "virgin birth" of Jesus Christ, supposedly prophesied by Isaiah as follows: "Therefore the Lord himself shall give you a sign: Behold, a virgin shall conceive, and bear a son, and shall call his name Immanuel" (Isa. 7:14).

As Wheless points out, the Hebrew word used by Isaiah and translated "virgin" is *almah*, which does not signify "virgin" but means *a young woman of marriageable age,* not necessarily of intact virginity. The precise Hebrew word for virgin is *bethulah;* and throughout the *Old Testament* the word *almah* appears seven times, always signifying a young female. The word *bethulah* is used fifty times, and in all fifty cases it has the technical meaning of virginity!

Thus, despite all the laborious fictions contrived to make it appear that Christ was born of a virgin (that is, a sexual) mother, the prophet Isaiah was speaking merely of an *almah*—that is, a young woman of marriageable age. And despite the attempts of Matthew, Luke and other sex-negative religionists, the so-called "Virgin Mary" mother of Christ, wife of Joseph, did in fact *know* her husband Joseph *in the body,* genitally, and thus bore half a dozen brothers and sisters of Jesus: "his brethren, James, and Joses, and Simon, and Judas, and his sisters" (Matt. 13:55,56; Mark 6:2,3).

And this alleged "Virgin Birth" conceived of Mary by God utterly destroys the sworn oath of God which states: "The patriarch David. . . . Therefore being a prophet, and knowing that God had sworn with an oath to him [Psalm 132:11,12] that of the fruit of his loins according to the flesh, he would raise up Christ to sit on his throne" (Acts 2:22, 29,30). For Christ, being of "Virgin Birth" could in no way be considered "the fruit of David's loins according to the flesh"!!

And Christ's own mother and father (Mary and Joseph)

certainly did not consider their son as "God," for, in fact the family and friends of Jesus, because of his odd behavior, considered him *insane* (Mark 3:21): "And when his friends [margin: relatives] heard of it, they went out to lay hold on him: for they said, He is beside himself" (*New American Standard Bible*, "lost his senses").

Surely had Christ been born of a Virgin Mother who conceived "miraculously" without the aid or need for man, such an event would figure prominently in *all* of the Gospels. Yet Mark mentions no virgin birth; neither does John, who refers to Christ as "the Son of God" (John 1:34) in the sense that *all* men have "the power to become sons of God, even to them that believe on his name" (John 1:12,13).

HUMAN: ALL TOO HUMAN

Was Christ God or simply a man, a beautiful, wise and compassionate genital man? Was there only one "Christ"? Or can there be millions, billions of Christs? If, as religious fanatics claim, Christ was God, then he would have to display the attributes of God: omnipotence, omniscience, omnipresence.

We look to the words of Christ himself for the answer: "The living Father hath sent me, and I live by the Father" (John 7:57); and Paul corroborated this: "He liveth by the power of God" (2 Cor. 13:4). Christ denied his own omnipotence: "The Son can do nothing of himself. . . . I can of mine own self do nothing" (John 5:19,30). If Christ was omniscient, if he knew *everything*, then of his Second Coming would he know also: "But of that day and that hour knoweth no man, no, not the angels which are in heaven, neither the Son, but the Father" (Mark: 13,32). What additional occurrence was Christ totally ignorant of? He did not know that the fig tree was barren, because he cursed the barren fig tree, as "he came, if haply he might find anything thereon" (Mark 11:13).

If Christ was God, then he had *infinite wisdom,* which, as Wheless points out, is *absolute;* how then was it that Christ "increased in wisdom" (Luke 2:52)?

Was Jesus infinitely good? This he also denied: "Why callest thou me good? There is none good but one, that is God" (Mark 10:18).

So what therefore *is* Christ that men revere him so? Why does the image of Christ sustain such power to move humanity to struggle, to strive for good, to feel at least guilty at evil, to pray and continually hope in *Him?*

The single greatest failing of Joseph Wheless' criticism and commentary of the Bible is his total lack of understanding of suffering, struggling armored man. *Despite* his armor, *homo sapiens* is still capable of great and wondrous works. It is patently obvious that Wheless was glutted with biblical dogma from early childhood—surfeited to the point of chronic nausea; his personal disappointment with "God," his frustrations, his inner torments, and his underlying knowledge that despite the myth and dogma, God does indeed exist—all of this contributes to a bitter rage against religion, per se. He does not seek the seeds of truth in the brittle knots of Holy Writ. Instead, he swings his academic axe with a fanaticism as zealous as the hypocritical zealots he smashes into powdery dust.

Wheless makes no pretensions to creativity. His role is not to build, but to devastate. Nothing—but nothing—remains standing of the ancient religious myths. Wheless did not, could not, ask: "How is it possible that for centuries, millions of people could embrace, unthinkingly, such falsehoods? Could live, conduct their personal and social lives, and indoctrinate their children in such irrationalism!" He does not and cannot comprehend Christ as *the essence of Genital Man,* surrounded by the emotional plague, victimized by his own decency and goodness, and finally destroyed by the very ones he sought to help. He does not and cannot understand Christ as the unarmored infant, the "sap of Life," tormented, tortured, and finally crucified for being nothing more than Life itself. He does not and cannot comprehend "Christ" as the story of the Murder of Life Itself, as Reich revealed it in his book *The Murder of Christ*.

Wheless not only smashes the religious crutches of armored man, but also he demolishes the entire religious infirmary—ceilings, floors, walls, windows and alcoves. Nevertheless, the "foundation" remains—the antisexual, life-negating character structure of armored man. As long as man continues to raise armored infants and children, the mystical foundation of irrational religion will always give rise to religious fanaticism, designed to serve the crippled needs of crippled organisms. This Wheless could not have known, since knowledge of the sex-negative nature of *irrational* religion was not known and fully elucidated. Marx called religion "the opiate of the people." It remained for Reich to demonstrate clinically how sexual crippling gives rise to the *need* for such an opiate.

Nevertheless, Joseph Wheless has earned the right to be called *a genuine Judge Advocate of Truth*. That he is almost totally unknown to students, and especially "religious students" of the twentieth century, is the general fate of all great thinkers. But we, the Students of the Future, cannot, will not forget him.

THE EMOTIONAL PLAGUE VERSUS TRUTH

As Reich asserted, "Truth is immediate contact with reality." The history of the human race is one of continuous searching for truth, while at the same time such truth-seeking has been relentlessly obstructed and opposed. The Holy Church, specifically in its "Christian" guise, has often posed as the Advocate of Truth while it has shamefully persecuted truth-seekers, often to the death, and has banned and burned "heretical treatises" throughout the centuries.

Contrary to the contentions of Joseph Wheless, the Holy Church is not the single greatest Adversary of Truth. The Adversary of Truth—especially Natural Truth or Natural Law— is the *Emotional Plague of mankind:* "Neurotic, destructive irrationalism at work on the social scene" (Reich).

Sick, hateful, arrogant men in high positions of trust have always set themselves up as judges of what is true or false in their time. But such contemptuous arrogance is not the sole province of the Church—for the emotional plague has operated in every age, in every country, and in all fields of human striving for new knowledge. It is a disease of armored man himself.

According to theological dogma, only the Church has the power and the authority to determine truth: "Nothing is to be accepted save on the authority of scripture, since greater is the authority of scripture than all the powers of the human mind," says St. Augustine in his *De Genesis.* The Church Father St. Ambrose put it this way: "Moses opened his mouth and poured forth what God said to him."

In other words, don't observe Nature directly; don't ponder God's Natural Laws; don't engage in frivolous human experimentation; don't theorize over a body of hard-earned factual material—simply read the Scriptures, and all will be revealed!

Moses, inspired by "God," stated that the Earth was flat and square, with "four corners." What more need we know? Therefore Columbus and Magellan were insufferable heretics to claim the rotundity of the patently flat, four-cornered Earth, conceived and populated in six days.

Copernicus, a greater prophet and truer soothsayer than any biblical prophet or pope, wrote his immortal "The Revolutions of the Heavenly Bodies," thereby, posthumously, incurring the wrath of the Holy Fathers who dogmatically denied that the sun was the center of the solar system, and that the Earth and other planets revolve around it. The Roman Church immediately denounced Copernicus' work as heresy, banning and suppressing its publication "until his statement should be corrected" to conform to the Bible and to the pagan Ptolemy. (In reading the twentieth century FDA Injunction against Wilhelm Reich and Orgonomy, one finds the same impassioned, baseless denunciations expressed again with ruthless arrogance. The emotional plague has not changed its methods or expressions one iota in man's miserable history!)

Luther also raged at Copernicus: "This fool wishes to reverse the entire science of astronomy; but sacred scripture tells us that Joshua commanded the sun to stand still, and not the earth."* In his "Commentary on Genesis," Calvin denounced all those misguided ones who believed that the Earth is not the center of the Universe, referring to Psalm 18:1: "The world also is established, that it cannot be moved!" And Calvin thundered: "Who will put the authority of Copernicus above that of the Holy Spirit?" John Wesley, the founder of Methodism, stated that such new ideas "tend toward infidelity."

In 1618 and 1619, the immortal Kepler published his "Epitome of the Copernican System" and "The Harmonies of the World." He was attacked by the Protestant Consistory of Stuttgart and solemnly admonished "not to throw Christ's kingdom into a confusion with his silly fancies." And Kepler was ordered to "bring his theory of the world into harmony with scripture"!

Giordano Bruno, a student of the Copernican system,

---

*Much of this material is based upon *History of the Warfare of Science with Theology*, by Andrew D. White, New York: D. Appleton & Co., 1925, and in the remarkable compendium, "Great Men in Conflict with the Emotional Plague," by Walter Hoppe, M.D., Vol. 3, Nos. 1 & 2: *Orgone Energy Bulletin*, Orgone Institute Press, Orgonon, Maine, 1951.

upon order of the Holy Church, spent seven years in filthy dungeons for daring to write his immortal satire ridiculing it, "The Expulsion of the Triumphant Beast." Since his imprisonment did not appear to change Bruno's "heretical views," both he and his books were consigned to the purifying flames of the Holy Inquisition in 1600 in Rome.

The magnificent Galileo was haled before the Inquisition by command of Pope Urban VIII, threatened with torture and flung into prison, and was finally made to recant, "abjuring and detesting the infamous doctrine of the earth's motion and the sun's stability." This occurred July 22, 1633.

The ancient Greeks—long before the Pillars of the Holy Christian Church were implanted—displayed the same fanatical intolerance for any new idea, any new thoughts which stirred men to think in ways contrary to those established by sick, armored society. Thus Pythagoras was denounced and died in exile; Socrates was forced to commit suicide; Plato lived in exile; Aristotle died in exile; the writings of Protagoras were burned; and Democritus was almost totally sequestered for his writings.

The great Jewish luminaries, Maimonides and Benedict Spinoza were both denounced and ridiculed by their Jewish contemporaries.

Vesalius, the father of anatomy, was denounced by his fellow physicians. He was hounded from country to country, and finally, in anger and despair, he destroyed all of his manuscripts and discontinued his study of anatomy.

Anton Leeuwenhoek, inventor of the microscope, worked almost entirely alone for twenty years. His neighbors and friends considered him insane.

The great French philosopher Voltaire was publicly and officially cursed and villified and confined to prison and then banished because of his writing. The German philosopher Immanuel Kant underwent a similar fate. He died impoverished and isolated.

Edward Jenner's announcement of vaccination was scorned by the Royal Society, since smallpox was considered "a visitation from God."

Faraday, Galvani, and Coulomb, all scientific fathers of modern-day electronics, met with misfortune and ridicule because of their work. Coulomb was jailed; Galvani lost his source of income; and Faraday was treated with cool contempt by his "fellow scientists."

The first mechanical loom invented by Joseph Jacquard went up in flames in Lyon because workers believed it would lead to mass unemployment. Phillippe de Girard met nothing but misfortune after inventing a machine that could spin linen. A similar fate was encountered by William Lee, who built the first practical knitting machine for hosiery. He died of starvation.

The majority of the scientific fraternity ridiculed John Ericsson's invention of the first screw propeller. The inventor suffered chronic poverty, and was imprisoned in London's debtors' prison.

The story of the discovery and suffering of Dr. Ignaz Philipp Semmelweis was immortalized in Morton Thompson's *The Cry and the Covenant* (New York: Garden City Books, 1949). Semmelweis discovered the cause of childbirth fever: Pregnant mothers and newborn babies were dying by the thousands because of the filth on the hands of the attending doctors. Semmelweis recommended washing the hands with an antiseptic. His colleagues refused, calling him "insane." After years of opposition and struggle against his contemptuous colleagues, Semmelweis committed suicide.

No country, no "race," and no "religion" are immune to the scourge of the emotional plague. In Germany, the scientist Robert Mayer, who founded the law of the preservation of energy, was sentenced to an insane asylum for his work. Duhrssen, who demonstrated the Caesarean section, was dismissed from his post at the University of

Berlin. In 1861, Phillip Reiss gave a public demonstration of his invention of the telephone, but could not get his articles published in scientific journals. Philosophers such as Goethe, Heine, and Schopenhauer were either publicly denounced or isolated.

The emotional plague in Russia—now fully organized as Communism—imprisoned its greatest writers, including Turgenev and Dostoyevsky, and God only knows how many other artists, writers, and poets in "modern-day" Russia.

In the United States, Walt Whitman died virtually penniless. His friend Emerson was "embarrassed" by Whitman's openhanded references to human love and sexuality. Whitman was forced to typeset and publish his own works, and few would read them. Whitman lost his government job when Secretary of the Interior James Harlan "searched" into Whitman's private belongings and discovered a manuscript of poems.

In France, Emile Zola, who fought the French government in his attempt to free the railroaded Captain Dreyfus, had to flee his native country. He was repeatedly branded "immoral," and was so poor that he was forced to trap and eat sparrows.

In Australia, Sister Kenny's innovative treatment of poliomyelitis led to a bitter 30-year struggle to suppress her work. In 1944, the AMA condemned her method as "ineffective and detrimental."

And on . . . and on . . . and on! And we have scarcely scratched the surface. But what is plain is that the pandemic illness, the emotional plague, is not confined to any nation, creed, or social stratum. Sick "brothers and sisters" join with sick "brothers and sisters" in destroying truth and fact in a tacit conspiracy to do what? To kill *truth*—specifically *any truth dealing with Nature and Natural Law!!* Thus *insane homo sapiens*, sticking like lice to the dead carcass of a morbid, savage, factless "religion," simultaneously fights with fang and claw any and every attempt to bring him into direct and immediate contact with his true "God"—the Life Energy both inside and outside his own body!

As Reich so aptly stated the problem: It is not that the orgone exists, but that mankind for millennia *has evaded contact with it!* Would true Children of God continually refuse to *know* the Father of Man? It is all too easy and illusionary to toss off this *evasion of the essential* by saying "humanity is evil—from birth, just as the Bible tells us." Infants are not *born* evil. If God is good, then his "fruit" must also be good, for no good tree beareth evil fruit. It is the hatred, the bitter, venomous hatred that armored man has for Life that perverts the good into the evil. It is the mishandling of infants by hateful adults that changes the gentle orgone energy in infants and children into a killer-energy. Specifically, it is the chronic inability of Dead Life to permit Living Life to *know* God as the streaming of Love in the genitals. The suppression and frustration of healthy heterosexual love is the *fons et origo* of the emotional plague.

Now, how do we stop it? How do we stop this chronic Murder of Christ, once and for all? We stop it first in ourselves, in our individual lives. We clean up the mess that has been made of our own lives by ignorant and hateful parents and educators. And if we cannot do this ourselves, then we must seek competent professional help.

Then we must stop the emotional plague by Fighting for Life, particularly where our own infants and children are concerned. We affirm and protect the child's Basic Right to Life and Love. This is the only kind of "revolutionary work" that is rational. How the infant and child experience genital gratification, whether pleasurably or filled with anxiety and fear—these are crucial to the individual's welfare, to society's welfare.

Still—still, you say, it is all too simple, too pat; and you will evade the essential by looking for the seed of man's misery in linguistics, in occultism, in esoteric philosophy, in economics. And this very same *evasion of the essential is,* as Reich showed, the greatest single tool of the emotional plague. You will make a heroine out of a Patty Hearst and overlook the millions of potential Patty Hearsts whose loving genitality is every day being converted, *radicalized* into frenzies of silent rage and impotence in the nursery and the classrooms of our world, to explode finally and violently against the very "Establishment" which your evasions build and support. *YOU are the Establishment! The "Government" always is and always will be the very individual people whose Life Energy and work and money support it!*

"DIVINELY INSPIRED CONSISTENCY" OF THE GOSPELS

All that man knew, for many hundreds of years, concerning the life and times of Jesus Christ was derived from four short monographs called "gospels"—meaning, in the Greek language, "good news."

Relying again upon the laborious and trenchant scholarship of Judge Advocate Joseph Wheless, we are guided by his firm hand and accurate eye in demonstrating that the so-called "eternal verities" are shot through with flagrant contradictions, unsupportable embellishments and omissions, and perplexing inaccuracies.

If four "witnesses" were to appear before a court of law in order to testify to the truth of specific events, and if one contradicted the other three, or two gave crucial evidence not verified by the others, or all four could not agree on major issues, then such testimony would be highly questionable, prejudicial and damaging to the cause of such witnesses.

A major attribute of the long-awaited Jewish Messiah was that he should come from the house and lineage of King

David. If Jesus was in truth this awaited Messiah, then his descent in unbroken line from King David must be established. Matthew begins his biography with "The book of the generation of Jesus Christ, the son of David, the son of Abraham" (Matt. 1:1). Matthew traces the lineage of Jesus by starting with Abraham, through a direct line of "begettings" to David, and from David, through Solomon and Roboam, to Jacob: "And Jacob begat Joseph the husband of Mary, of whom was born Jesus, who is called Christ" (Matt. 1:16).

Then, Matthew specifically states that from David to Christ there are twenty-eight generations (1:17). Here, then, is Matthew's "divinely-inspired" genealogy tracing the direct descent of Jesus from David:

Matthew's Genealogy (1:6-16)

1. David	15. Jechonias
2. Solomon	16. Salathiel°
3. Roboam	17. Zorobabel°
4. Abia	18. Abiud
5. Asa	19. Eliakim°
6. Josaphat	20. Azor
7. Joram	21. Sadoc
8. Ozias	22. Achim
9. Joatham	23. Eliud
10. Achaz	24. Eleazar
11. Ezekias	25. Matthan
12. Manasses	26. Jacob
13. Amon	27. Joseph
14. Josias	28. Jesus

In his equally inspired biography of Jesus Christ, Luke starts his genealogical tabulations in reverse order—that is,

---

°Indicates names occurring in both lists.

from Jesus to David, instead of from David to Jesus as in
Matthew's tale. Luke's version establishes *forty-three* generations from David to Jesus, compared to Matthew's
twenty-eight. Note well also that when we compare both
lists, *only three names on the two contradictory lists are the
same,* excepting David on one end of the lists and Joseph
and Jesus on the other end. Here, then, is Luke's inspired
tabulation:

Luke's Genealogy (3:23-31)

1. David	23. Zorobabel°
2. Nathan	24. Rhesa
3. Mattatha	25. Joanna
4. Menan	26. Juda
5. Melea	27. Joseph
6. Eliakim°	28. Semei
7. Jonan	29. Mattathias
8. Joseph	30. Maath
9. Juda	31. Nagge
10. Simeon	32. Esli
11. Levi	33. Naum
12. Matthat	34. Amos
13. Jorim	35. Mattathias
14. Eliezer	36. Joseph
15. Jose	37. Janna
16. Er	38. Melchi
17. Elmodam	39. Levi
18. Cosam	40. Matthat
19. Addi	41. Heli
20. Melchi	42. Joseph
21. Neri	43. Jesus
22. Salathiel°	

°Indicates names occurring in both lists.

If, as we believe, truth can set men free, then it is time to cut away the falsehoods of self-proclaimed prophets and "disciples of God." A comparison of the two genealogies proves that either one or both of these "truth-sayers" were wrong. Moreover, if Jesus was *not* the procreated son of Joseph, but was rather the incarnate offspring of Yahveh and the virgin Mary, then he could not possibly be a human or blood descendant of David! Thus, in no way could Jesus be the "Son of David."

Later, Jesus denied that he was the son of David. According to the inspired scribes of the gospels, "While the Pharisees were gathered together, Jesus asked them, Saying, What think ye of Christ? whose son is he? They say unto him, The son of David. He saith unto them, How then doth David in spirit call him Lord? . . . If David then call him Lord, how is he his son?" (Matt. 22:41-43,45; Mark 12:35-37; Luke 20:41-44). Nobody could answer this question.

We have touched briefly upon the perpetual virginity of Jesus' mother, Mary. The dogma of chastity, of asexuality, is constantly fabricated and perpetuated by sex-negating armored prelates and celibates. Mary did indeed *know* Joseph sexually, and bore several children, brothers and sisters of Jesus: "his brethren, James and Joses, and Simon, and Judas, and his sisters" (Matt. 13:55,56; Mark 6:2,3); and Paul declares that he saw his friend the apostle "James the Lord's brother" (Gal. 1:19).

The four inspired gospel-writers cannot tell one event simply or entirely without contradicting each other, no matter how earth-shaking the event might have been. Judge Wheless cites hundreds of such contradictions; however, we shall now consider only a relatively small number of the more outstanding incidents and episodes in the life of Jesus, described by his closest associates in their four disparate gospel renditions.

Matthew claims that Jesus cured Peter's mother-in-law

after he cleansed the leper (Matt. 8:2,3,14,15). But Mark and Luke flatly contradict this (Mark 1:29-31; 40-42; Luke 4:38-39; 5:12, 13).

Was the leper himself cleansed *after* the Sermon on the Mount, as Matthew would have it? (5:1; 8:1-4). Or *before* the Sermon, as Luke claims (5:12-14)?

In the healing of the centurion's servant, did the centurion come to Jesus for help (Matt. 8:5) or did he send Jewish elders (Luke 8:2-4)?

Did the miraculous healing of the centurion's servant occur in Capernaum, as Matthew states (8:5) and Luke corroborates (8:1)? Or was it performed in Cana, as noted by John (4:46)?

When ordering his disciples on their first crusade, Jesus commanded them to "take neither shoes nor yet staves" according to two of the gospel writers: (Matt. 10:9,10; Luke 10:3). But then Mark says he commanded them to take shoes and staves and nothing else (Mark 6:8,9).

In the renowned miracle wherein the multitude was fed, were the loaves and fishes provided by the disciples (Matt. 14:15-17; Mark 6:35-38; and Luke 9:12,13)? If so, why then does John say the loaves and fishes were donated by "a lad" (John 6:9)?

After the miracle of the loaves and fishes, what happened? According to two writers, Jesus "sent the multitude away" (Matt. 14:22; Mark 6:45). According to another, he did not send them away, but withdrew himself into a mountain (John 6:15).

Jesus ordered his disciples, after feeding the multitude, to set sail "unto Bethsaida" (Mark 6:45). So they dutifully steered a course "toward Capernaum" (John 6:17) and thus came "into the land of Genesaret" (Matt. 14:34).

If a great man were going to his death, would his closest associates know in what place that man made his last prayer? Christ made his last prayer in the Garden of

Gethsemane, state Matthew 26:36,39; Mark 14:32,35; and Luke 22:39,41. But John records that Jesus' last prayer was made in Jerusalem, before he went to Gethsemane (John 17; 18:1).

Now we arrive at one of the most moving events in the lives of the disciples—the crucifixion of Jesus. Of the exact inscription reportedly placed above the head of the crucified Jesus, we find the following accounts:

"And [the soldiers who crucified Christ] set up over his head his accusation written, This is Jesus the King of the Jews." (Matt. 27:37).

Mark, however, notes: "And the superscription of his accusation was written over, The King of the Jews" (Mark 15:26).

Luke saw it this way: "And a superscription also was written over him in letters of Greek, and Latin, and Hebrew, This is the King of the Jews" (Luke 23:38).

But John's version states: "And Pilate wrote a title and put it on the cross. And the writing was, Jesus of Nazareth, the King of the Jews" (John 19:19). But then John, who claims he was present throughout this incident, adds further confusing material: "Then said the chief priests of the Jews to Pilate, Write not, The King of the Jews; but that he said, I am King of the Jews. Pilate answered, What I have written I have written" (John 19:21).

And in the final seconds of the agony of Christ, what were the last words spoken by Jesus and subsequently recorded by his gospel-writing disciples? Matthew and Mark both mention hearing the same anguished cry: *"Eli, Eli, lama sabachthani"*—a repetition of David's heartfelt plea (Psalm 22:1) "My God, My God, why hast thou forsaken me?"

Luke doesn't mention this rending cry, but records instead a remark Jesus made to one of the thieves crucified beside him (23:43): "To-day shalt thou be with me in paradise." And then in the ninth hour, the dying words, "Father, into thy hands I commend my spirit" (Luke 23:46). John relates two remarks made by the dying Jesus with respect to John and the mother of Jesus: "Woman, behold thy son!" and to John, "Behold thy mother!" and, finally, "I thirst" (John 19:26-28). And, with his last breath, Christ exclaimed, "It is finished: and he bowed his head and gave up the ghost" (John 19:30).

Moreover, after the death of Jesus, the discrepancies and contradictions of the gospel writers continue unabated. If we study the details of the burial of the martyred Christ we find the following:

Matthew tells us that when even was come, a rich disciple of Jesus, one Joseph of Arimathea, "went to Pilate, and begged the body of Jesus" (Matt. 27:58).

But in Mark's version, Joseph didn't "beg" the body, but "went in boldly unto Pilate, and craved the body of Jesus" (15:43).

According to John, however, Joseph neither "begged" for Jesus' body, nor did he go in "boldly"—but *secretly* for fear of the Jews, besought Pilate" (19:38).

Now, after the body was prepared for burial, according to Matthew, Joseph "rolled a great stone to the door of the sepulchre, and departed" (27:60), and he left two Marys "sitting over against the sepulchre" (27:61; Mark 15:46,47). Yet Luke informs us that Joseph, though alone, did not roll a stone against the door, but simply laid the body of Jesus inside (23:53) and departed, and there is no mention of two Marys or any other women watching. And after Joseph had left the scene, "the women . . . followed after, and beheld the sepulchre, and how his body was laid" (23:55), which details they could not have seen had a stone blocked the doorway of the sepulchre.

Then, after Christ's burial and ascension, the disciples continue their "inspired" disagreements over doctrine. How, for example, are we to regard circumcision? This question is debated and dodged, as Wheless shows, in the following manner:

According to Acts 15:

> Is any man called being circumcised? let him not become uncircumcised. Is any called in uncircumcision? Let him not be circumcised. Circumcision is nothing, and uncircumcision is nothing, but the keeping of the commandments of God. (1 Cor. 7:18, 19)

Paul takes issue with this assertion: "For circumcision verily profiteth, if thou keep the law" (Rom. 2:25), and then contradicts both of these statements: "Behold, I Paul say unto you, that if ye be circumcised, Christ shall profit you nothing" (Gal. 5:2). And this same Paul proceeds to deny this very dictum, by asserting: "What profit is there of circumcision? Much every way" (Rom. 3:1,2). And, finally, contradicts himself yet again: "For in Jesus Christ neither circumcision availeth any thing, nor uncircumcision" (Gal. 5:6).

So, let us leave the inspired writers of the Gospels of Jesus Christ and turn our attention to the cornerstone of Christian religious fanaticism, the doctrine of Damnation and Salvation.

Wherever men and women live happy, healthy lives; wherever Love, Work and Knowledge rule—or will rule—our Earth, there shall you find no need for Salvation, because loving, happy, healthy people are indeed "saved" from the DOR that is "sin," sickness, and the principle of Death.

The Christian fanatic preaches that all men are damned from the beginning. Without damnation, what need for salvation? If mankind is *not* damned, then the entire thrust and scope (and attractiveness) of Christian inharmonies cannot and will not take root.

Unhappy, miserable, sexually-frustrated armored man

requires the substitute contact of "God" to replace the rational Paradise of happiness here and now on Earth which he has lost. Armored man feels "evil," and dirty; he feels vile and lustful. And so he yearns for cleanliness "in Heaven," which is the liberation from his engulfing armor. Thus armored man preaches and teaches the "Doctrine of Original Sin," the fall of Adam and Eve in the Garden of Eden, and the subsequent punishment by God, the curse of eternal damnation and hellfire, unless sinful man gains salvation through Jesus Christ.

Yet Jesus Christ never mentioned Adam or the stupendous curse and the "Fall of Man." Nowhere in the New Testament does Christ suggest that his mission on Earth was to absolve the curse given by God to a talking snake in the Garden of Eden. Nor does any one of the gospel writers mention such a curse, or the need for redemption for any sin of Adam.

Christ, in truth, is healthy, rational genital love—the greatest single gift of God to you, His children.

IS GOD DEAD?

No, God is not dead; and the world itself gives proof of a million daily miracles. That you breathe, and eat, walk and talk, love and think—these are all miraculous events. Your search for Truth in all things is itself the highest expression of God in humanity. The Life Energy constantly presses to "know itself," to merge with the Creative Wellspring from whence it came. Your longing, your sadness, your ecstatic happiness and deepest sorrow, your *rational* anxiety and anger, the glow of love you feel for your mate, these are expressions of God in you and you in God.

For the Students of the Future, the ancient, vengeful, patriarchal God of Moses and Paul *is* dead! Brilliant minds like Nietzsche and Wheless have ripped the hypocrisy and deceit from such anthropoid gods. Yet such gods have not died; they continue to exist and persist in the armor of distorted mankind. Since the armor never changes, the concept of a moralistically compulsive god does not change. Armored man requires a patriarchal, sex-negating, bellowing, fire-and-brimstone-spewing god: it is the projected, the ultimate image of feared father to more fearful Father. Hence Caesar; hence Hitler.

I recall back in the early 1940s, at New York University, in our philosophy classes we would argue for or against the "existence of God." Everything has a cause, therefore the universe must have had a cause—*ergo*, God. ("But, if everything has a cause, what then 'caused' God?") Lay *that* one on your old man when he gets home from the office! In your late teens and early twenties, of course, you realize that you suddenly have the answers to everything. You're so brilliant! And so damnably miserable!

You take an axe, a rifle, a sack of flour, salt and some sugar, and backpack into the deep woods of northern Idaho, back into the untouched wilderness. There you clear the land, build a cabin, plant or transplant trees and wild greens and other edibles, erect a smokehouse, dig a root cellar, stack wood for your fireplace. You've built your "paradise." You've built your Universe. I come along and inquire: "Who built this little heaven on Earth?" Since everything must have a cause, then your little Paradise must have a cause. *You* caused it—built the cabin, the root cellar, the fireplace, the table and chairs. Is it necessary to know who created *you* in order to know who built your house?

The computer-minded mechanical robots who pass for "teachers" hedge and dodge the question by the very way they ask it. So we must pin them down to specifics. We ask for a definition, a strict definition of God. We forget the Bible now; we forget theology, scripture, rituals, and the so-called holy writs of a thousand supposedly sacrosanct books scribbled by the fiery finger of "god." We simply ask for a definition of God.

God is the creative power of the universe. Is that not correct? God must be everywhere—not just in a gold-plated temple, but in a poor man's tarpaper shack, a prison cell, a submarine under water, on the moon, on Venus—*everywhere*. It is this selfsame "God" that creates life, a tree, sunlight, rain, tornadoes, silkworms, sperm cells and ova, fish, elephants, brain cells, testicles and wombs, hair, toenails, crows and eagles. It is this selfsame God that is responsible for instinct, for emotions, for knowing when you're hungry and thirsty, for regulating or exciting your heartbeat, for circulating your blood.

Again, it is this selfsame "God" that is the "Father" of redman and blackman and yellow man, of white babies and brown babies. The selfsame God. It is again this selfsame God that heals the cut on your big toe, moves you to feeling alive and in love, to glow with life and exuberance. It is this "God" moving through your limbs, genitals and belly that is your *emotions*. It is again this selfsame God that is the creative power of your inspirations (where do they come from, nowhere?) that fills you with sadness and longing, joy and happiness, the desire to feel more, to know more, to expand and embrace your mate, your infant, the world.

And what is the power, the Life Force, the creative energy that functions at the base of all these things—it is indeed the scintillating, streaming, thrillingness of the orgone in your body which is in fact the God of which we speak, which we seek; and which, not finding, we destroy ourselves for, in misery, in isolated armoring, in frenzies of striving to find "salvation."

Salvation—we all seek salvation. And what is salvation? How are we *saved*? Saved from what for what? From sin? We want salvation from sin? Choked, stifled, chained in our armored bodies, the core-alive, living life craves "salvation" —freedom from sin, from DOR, from stagnation and decay.

So, God is not dead, never was, never will be. Armored man in his deadness feels dead and feels that therefore his god must be dead, else why does armored man remain armored, remain dead? Armored man prays bitterly and ceaselessly and cries, *"Jesus, save me! I am saved in Jesus!"* But armored man still feels sinful, dirty, armored—still feels trapped, cut off from Heaven (which is the ability, the capacity to know real love) and thus cannot ever be truly saved.

God is not dead—no. And the epitome of God in man, Jesus Christ, is not dead either, since Christ continues to be born in every single baby born to man on Earth. As Reich showed, armored man continuously murders Christ—the ability to live and love—in every newborn babe; and so, crucified in the nursery, in the crib, in schools and orphanages, in juvenile delinquency homes, armored man grows up knowing the scars of crucifixion in his own body. So we seek the mirror-image of Jesus Christ, we seek the genital love, the real tender physical gratification we cannot enjoy —we seek it, forever, endlessly, elusively—in drugs, in communes, in booze, in rigid, lascivious gyrations we call "dance," in cults of Witchcraft, Satanism, and Lust—all, all being the same essential masked face of "God," the lost God of babyhood, infancy and childhood.

Whether you embrace a Symbionese Revolutionary Movement or a Jesus Freak Commune philosophy—what you are looking for is your lost love, your once-healthy genitality, crippled now and on crutches. You desire above all, healthy, full genital pleasure. I said, *healthy genital pleasure!* If you had *that*, if you just once could love your mate *fully and completely*, with the ecstatic satisfaction God created in mankind to enjoy, you would know in your guts what I am talking about.

We wouldn't then have to discuss what "God" is—because you would know God, immediately and fully, and you would protect and safeguard that *knowing* of God in your own infants and children, and in your adolescents. And you would fight like hell any decaying, shriveled spinster or beady-eyed plaguey blackguard who attempted to make your child feel guilty about his or her natural, healthy, primary heterosexual needs and pleasures!

You would know that there is a War against Life which has been going on for thousands of years, and that the price of happiness comes very high: You have to fight for it, daily, hourly. You have to guard Life, guard the living, and constantly affirm the healthy genitality of your child, as the child's God-given birthright! *And if you do not fight the plague; if you don't stand up for your own happiness, if you do not forsake mother and father and cleave unto "Me," which is your God-given genital love, then you are not worthy of the Life and Love God gave you at your creation!*

You, Students of the Future, will have to be tougher than the plague you fight, and still retain your sensitivity and decency, and still keep your love-life clean and wholesome. That will be quite a task, quite a job.

But you will have fact and truth on your side, and the profound security of knowing you are on the side of Life, not of Death. And you will have, eternally, my hopes, and love, and all my prayers and blessings.

NATURAL LAW

Natural Law governs the universe. It is the direct expression of God. If man lives in harmony with this law then the opportunities for a happy existence are limitless. If we, out of ignorance or malice, live contrary to Natural Law, then we truly create a hell on earth. The great struggles of great thinkers and scientists throughout history were simply attempts to grasp and define Natural Law. It is part of the Natural Law itself to give the impetus to mankind to find and know such a law.

In ancient Greece, the Stoics attempted to uncover Natural Law as the basis for their moral philosophy. When we consider morality, as such, we are always considering *sexual* morality.

The Romans were practical thinkers, given to logical thinking. The word logical is derived from "logos," *the law*. Thus, the great minds of the centuries sought constantly to uncover "the law." What is the best way to conduct one's life? The Romans took over the Greek philosophy of Stoicism (Cf: *Legacy of Freedom*, by George Charles Roche III, New York, Arlington House, 1969.)

Cicero was one of the most prominent social thinkers of ancient Rome. He asserted in *De Finibus* ("Concerning the Purpose of Life"):

> . . . the Chief Good consists in applying to the conduct of life a knowledge of the working of natural causes, choosing what is in accordance with nature and rejecting what is contrary to it; in other words, the Chief Good is to live in agreement and in harmony with nature.

"True law," Cicero stated, "is right reason in agreement with nature." Marcus Aurelius advocated the "Natural Life," a life that "consists for every creature in a strict conformity with the essential principle of that creature's constitution."

During the historical period known as the Age of Reason (roughly between 1650 and the 1800s) man became infatuated with his ability to reason, to think. What can a man know for certain? Descartes asked himself: "I think, therefore I exist." The functionalist of today, however, might better declare: "I *feel*, therefore I exist," since thought is based upon the movement of biological energy, and energy movement is functionally identical with feeling.

Kepler, Galileo, Descartes, Newton, Rousseau—all were seeking some fundamental insight into Natural Law. There was a powerful struggle between those who, correctly, sought to know *man himself* by first studying Nature, and those who, fearing Nature, the Living in Nature, recoiled into the static-absolute of "moral law"—hence religious law and sex-negation.

Simultaneously, there was always the fear of persecution, and the deep and abiding longing for Truth and Justice. To whom could one appeal in matters of lies and *injustice?* To the King? The State? How does one define what is "true" and "good" and "natural" and "rational," if there is no objectively verifiable Natural Law, no "Heavenly Court" of Appeal?

The acceptance of the Bible as "the word of God" opened at least an avenue of appeal. But, as we have seen in previous sections of this book, the same religious fanatics who professed "God's Law" became the foremost oppressors of Truth and Justice.

Still, still . . . man-made law was often capricious, malevolent and contrary to the best interests of humanity and society. Armored man proved, time and again, that he was evil, lazy, incapable of freedom, and therefore required and submitted to a ruler, a king, a dictator.

Unless man had some objectively verifiable basis for comprehending factually what "God" and "Natural Law" are, the tug-of-war between oppressor and oppressed continued through the ages of man's misery and struggle.

To understand the true nature of man required an understanding of the truth regarding Nature itself. Time and again, as Reich demonstrated, man erroneously reasoned *from man* to Nature, instead of the other way around: *from Nature to man!*

The fear to *touch* Nature, to *know* Nature, to *make contact* with Nature is the built-in taboo of armored man's rigid musculature. The Inquisition in every age is armored man's anxiety and hatred over touching one's genitals with pleasure. If you cannot love genitally, with full pleasure, then you are living the crippled, crooked life of armored existence. Therefore you will tend to avoid truth. And, as the emotional plague, you will torture and destroy anyone who seeks to bring you into contact with truth and Natural Law.

But the equation: Man-made Law should equal Natural Law, was never lost. The great jurist, Blackstone, wrote:

> *Natural Law, being coeval with mankind, and dictated by God himself is, of course, superior in obligations to any other. It is binding over all the globe, in all countries, and at all times. No human laws are of any validity, if contrary to this; and such of them as are valid derive their authority, mediately or immediately, from the original.*

To be rational (i.e., in conformance with truth and fact), human laws, codes of conduct and avenues by which to gain justice, must accord with Natural Law. Whatever is contrary to Natural Law, regardless of the law's age or number of supporters, is automatically null and void.

Pulsation is a basic *natural* lawfulness of the living organism. Therefore whatever impedes or frustrates pulsation in the living organism, infant, child, adolescent is contrary to Nature. Cutting off the foreskin of a baby boy in conformance with ancient, barbaric Talmudic "Law" severely damages and cripples the baby's pulsation! It is therefore a practice clearly contrary to Natural Law—irrational and life-negative! Punishing children for feeling their genital pulsations, and denying them their right to know (*touch*) their genitals, is again contrary to Natural Law! Furthermore, since it is Naturally Lawful for the Life Energy *in Nature* to superimpose and merge, the superimposition and merger of two adolescents in the genital embrace must likewise be naturally lawful. *It must be affirmed and protected!*

If it can be demonstrated that a certain chemical or drug in social use damages the pulsatory functions of the living cell or organism, then such chemical or drug, or "food" or "drink" should be treated accordingly.

When it is demonstrated that certain forms of man-made energy, such as nuclear energy, radiation, X-rays, TV sets, fluorescent lights, radar and laser beams, or industrial chemicals and by-products have a deleterious effect upon the Life Energy in Nature and humanity, then they must be withdrawn or replaced by agents which are not noxious and killing.

Now—can you begin to understand why I say that Reich's objectification of the Natural Law is so vitally important, so necessary for the building of healthy, rational people and a good social structure?

All space is filled with energy. It must be filled with either Life-positive or Life-negative energy, with the orgone or DOR. Ideas, ideologies represent states of energy in the human animal. The destruction of *"religion"* cannot leave an energy vacuum. The brutal atheism of Communism is a grotesque and distorted ideology that fills the "emptiness" of the Godless Soviet masters. For the mechanistic mind of today, "science" *is* the religion, ruthless in its inability to permit functional life or thought to exist. And the mystical religionist is, basically, just as mechanistically rigid in his intolerance and hatred for Natural Law.

Thanks to Wilhelm Reich, for the first time in human history mankind has stepped out of mechanism and mysticism into functionalism. We have only begun our lessons in this Cosmic Kindergarten. Let us enter with good hope and humility.

ON THE STAGE

For many, many months in 1974, two social dramas captured the interest of millions: Watergate and the Symbionese Liberation Army. In the former we see the corruption,

conniving and spying of the emotional plague in the highest
political offices of the United States; in the latter, the living
fantasies of every teenager played out in three-dimensional
life, with Patty Hearst, daughter of millionaire Randolph
Hearst, in the role of "heroic revolutionary and fighter for
freedom." Both dramas are tragedies.

We must look for the common functioning principle
governing both dramas. In the Watergate Mess, we are
confronted with the lurid and shabby spectacle of highly
educated and once-respected men of intellect, authority,
and money engaging in conspiracies, flaunting the rights of
others, hiding, spying, and condoning and aiding such
nefarious acts in others. What is at issue here is simply
immorality. And as I've said before, a person's *morals* are
based upon his sexual life—which means his capacity for
genital pleasure, genital health. The more sexually impotent
a politician is, the more will he seek *power* on the social
scene: *political power is perverted sexual gratification!* The
fact that politics, per se, is a field totally devoted to the
acquisition of power over human beings, demonstrates how
immoral (sexually ill) civilized man really is. War is always
the ultimate result of political machinations in times of
"peace." Students of history know full well that peace is an
illusion of armored man. There can be no "peace" for
armored man, except in the grave, for he is constantly at
war, with himself, with his wife, his children, his competi-
tors, his God.

In Reich's great volume *People in Trouble,* he reveals
how the muscular armoring of man—and *not* class, or race,
or wealth or poverty—is the divisive factor that pits worker
against worker, Protestant against Catholic, wife against husband, child against parents. To say that Capitalism is against
Labor, that Rich are against Poor, that Workers are always
downtrodden, etc., etc., is a speciously contrived argument
to turn attention *away* from the common functioning principle of man's perennial miseries—*armored man himself!*

Sociologists delighted in telling us that crime was the handmaiden of poverty. And there are elements of truth here. To steal bread to feed hungry children, when there is no work and no way to "lawfully" gain bread, is no "crime" in my book. But what of the crimes of the Watergate conspirators? What of the deliberate murder of innocent people by wealthy, intellectually endowed, "educated" people, like some in the Symbionese Liberation Army? The SLA fights for what? For "freedom"? To "liberate" the masses? No— you do not build a new society by tactics of demolition, mayhem, murder, and arrogant disregard for innocent people.

What did the Watergate conspirators want? What did these secretive manipulators of files, of lists of names, of millions of dollars—what did they really want? They desired power—control over peoples' lives. They sought to destroy all elements that threatened their control. Had all of the machinations of Watergate been conducted in the Soviet Union, under the auspices of the KGB, we would not have been surprised. Watergate is a revelation to the Americans in that it discloses the seedbed of an *American* KGB. Politicians in *all* countries, like military chiefs and secret agents, are in reality brothers under the skin! (The magnificent European film *The Fifth Day of Peace* clearly reveals this.)

Patty Hearst could easily have become enmeshed in the Watergate web of subversion; but her irrational anxiety and anger had not completely solidified in her muscular armoring. What she did, and will continue to do (until the final act of her tragedy is played out), are overt, more direct expressions of her sexual frustrations.*

And so she will be lionized as a "freedom fighter" and a "hero of the revolution." What "revolution"? She is really screaming with rage to liberate *herself* from her own trap

*The references to Patricia Hearst were written nearly two years before her arrest, trial and conviction.

of armor; and she cannot do it, she will never be able to do it—not without competent orgonomic help.

Her struggle to "be free" on the stage of society is therefore the real-life drama of every adolescent youth everywhere in the world. They yearn for salvation and "liberation," which is sexual gratification; they consciously or unconsciously hate their parents, therefore the Establishment, therefore their Government, their Country and God. They identify with the oppressed, with convicts, the impoverished, the downtrodden, because they themselves feel oppressed, convicted, impoverished and downtrodden. Instead of working to build a better school, a better factory, a better farm, a better "political" system, and thus a better world, they take the road of destruction, killing, and total lawlessness.

Patty Hearst was never poor in the material sense—far from it. She represents the new breed of wealthy kids who go socially haywire. She had money, cars, the best schools— you name it. She had everything except the freedom to express her genital love in a healthy way. Since natural heterosexual love was *unlawful* for Patty Hearst, she took to overt lawless behavior in order to find such love.

But the frustrated-love element is never mentioned in news stories. Her parents, stunned and bewildered, grope for answers to her "brainwashed" behavior. Christ's parable of the sower is applicable here: *Seeds of hatred can only take firm root in ground that has been cultivated to nourish such hatred!*

What began as a purely pathological case of sexual frustration will end in a criminal courtroom or a grave. And millions of love-starved kids, bursting themselves with ungratified sexual energy, will hail her as "sister," "hero" and "martyr." What it boils down to, in adolescent minds, is simply this: Grab a gun, throw a grenade, and get a lover! Fight Daddy-the-Pig, in the guise of teacher, cop, preacher, or bank president, and get "turned on." (We must take seriously these expressions of youth: "turned on" means to *glow*, to feel love, no matter how perverse or distorted.) And the "revolutionary" kids can point with justification to Watergate and its sordid players as examples of deception and hypocrisy on the part of Big Daddy, the Establishment: "What the hell," they say, and truly, "the bastard politicians conscript us to get killed in meaningless wars, while they steal millions at home!"

Watergate and the SLA are expressions of twentieth-century man's frustrated genital life. In their extremes they inevitably lead to chaos, and thence to total dictatorship.

THE DOUBLE-SQUEEZE TECHNIQUE OF THE EMOTIONAL PLAGUE

The emotional plague is essentially a disease of social significance, defined and elaborated upon by Reich as "neurotic, destructive irrationalism at work on the social scene." Its most powerful tool is *evasion of the essential.* To put a stop to this chronic evasion of the essential, we must constantly place Life in the focus of our attention: *We focus on Life.*

The motive force of emotional-plague behavior is derived from the held and stale biological orgone energy in the human organism (DOR)—energy which has been converted from a life-positive force to a deadly killer by way of chronic muscular rigidities.

Emotional-plague characters are never aware of this pathological condition in themselves. (Cf: Reich's *Character Analysis* and E. F. Baker's *Man in the Trap.*) Motive, means, and goal are never consonant. Touching upon the motive for an emotional-plague action invariably elicits anger or anxiety from the plague carrier.

We find this pandemic illness in all areas and at all levels of society. Fascism of both the far Right and the far Left is a manifestation of the *socially organized* emotional plague— the greatest single man-made evil threatening peaceful self-regulated living on Earth.

The EP character uses every means of deceit, cunning, and ruthless force to obtain power and mastery over an individual, a group, a nation, or a planet. Conspiracy and conniving are part of his trademark. Where "persuasion" fails, a bullet will do. *He is totally committed to his goals!* (It is precisely this total commitment that attracts liberals to sympathize with an EP character. The ruthless use of power and simultaneous willingness to actually die for a cause create a magnetic attraction for the leftist liberal.) Until we have Students of the Future who are totally committed to the Cause of Life, the emotional plague will never be stamped out.

I want to elaborate here upon only one of the many effective techniques employed by the plague throughout the world—the "double-squeeze" technique. This technique, because of its widespread use, and because of the innocence of the victims involved, is generally evaded and "overlooked." Only by exposing the emotional plague to full public light can we hope to understand and stop it. Let us first see how this technique operates in the world of the child.

The typical pathological family structure is patriarchic, authoritarian and sex-negating. The eruption of pornography and sexual licentiousness in today's culture is just as sex-negating as yesteryear's prudishness. Where the latter was openly suppressive, the former is arrogantly contemptuous. Genital pleasure of a genuine nature cannot exist in either climate.

The child in such a stifling situation is always the victim. Whether the child actually lives at home or in a "state school" makes no essential difference— the mechanisms to be described occur by virtue of emotional-plague "parents" —actual or proxy.

Let us say that both parents want something from the child—perhaps conformance to an established house rule or the extraction of some information which the child is either reluctant or not able to supply. One parent invariably assumes the role of the "Figure of Sympathy." The other becomes the "Figure of Violence." These two ostensibly diametrically opposed forces have a common-functioning principle: *bitter hatred of the Living and the unappeasable desire to dominate by force!*

The Figure of Sympathy (mother or father, it makes no difference) says, "You know mommy loves you. She doesn't want to see you punished *by your father*. So why don't you do what mommy says —like a good child. *We* don't want to get father angry now, do we?"

At school, the same double-squeeze technique is used by the plague teacher who, assuming the role of Figure of Sympathy, says: "We wouldn't want the school principal to hear about this, would we?" Note well the false attitude of sympathetic understanding and secretive alliance that the Figure of Sympathy attempts to establish between himself and the victim *against* the Figure of Violence (father, God, principal, etc.).

Moving into the adult world, we find the exact same double-squeeze technique more overtly expressed, especially in Red and Black Fascist espionage work everywhere. Most frequently, interrogation teams employ the two plague-created figures. The Figure of Violence is ruthless in his interrogation of the victim. The victim may be starved, beaten, shocked and tortured to the edge of endurance by the Figure of Violence, whereupon he is confronted by the Figure of Sympathy, who offers surcease from pain, friendship, a cigaret, a sumptuous meal. The Figure of Sympathy will go so far as to denounce his partner of evil, scorning his "barbarism," his unbridled, contemptible sadism. The Figure of Sympathy always attempts to ally himself with the victim as confidant and fellow-sufferer. ("I'm not really a part of this horror. I don't want to see you killed. *For your own good,* trust me, cooperate. I'm your friend.")

This, in essence, is the technique of the Double Squeeze. Confronted alternately by the Figure of Violence and the Figure of Sympathy, American prisoners in Korea and Vietnam—and the victims of the organized plague everywhere—have succumbed. And where they did cooperate, there was still no escape.

In the arena of the political plague strategists (including "scientific" politicians) the exact same mechanisms are employed. When it comes to "gathering" information and "boring from within" no one exceeds the Red and Black Masters of Deceit!

A glaring example of this is revealed in *Psychic Discoveries Behind the Iron Curtain.*° The two young American authors of this book were typical innocents abroad. These two women, Sheila Ostrander and Lynn Schroeder, were taken on a whirlwind tour through Communist countries to meet with top Communist scientists engaged in psychic research. We must ask—Why? Why were these women invited behind the Iron Curtain to review and report? (One should also ask why American nuclear scientists, astronauts, businessmen and congressmen are encouraged "with open arms" to review and report?)

But to return to our ingenuous women travelers who were invited to an ESP conference in Moscow. Just as the conference got under way, the latest issue of *Pravda* (official Communist organ) appeared *with an attack on ESP re-*

°Published by Prentice-Hall, Inc., Englewood Cliffs, N.J., 1970.

search!!! Why does the official Soviet government invite people from all over the world to attend a conference and then attack the principles of this very same conference in an official government publication? Of course, it's "crazy." But there is calculated craftiness in this craziness.

Although Ostrander and Schroeder concede, *"Articles do not happen in the six-page daily by chance,"* they nonetheless fail to see their role in this fabricated display of "disapproval." The Communist ESP researchers regale the American writers with shocked indignation over *Pravda's* "attack."

"It's a vicious attack!" one of the official Red translators assigned to the Americans exclaims. "This article is full of lies. . . . It's all nonsense!" Thus the stage is artfully set for the Double Squeeze between the Figures of Sympathy (Soviet ESP researchers) and the terrible Figure of Violence (the nebulous Communist hierarchy).

At the ESP conference, in the shadow of the Kremlin, Dr. Vassili Efimov ominously warns Ostrander and Schroeder, "We must widen the consciousness of humanity. It is *vital* that the paranormal powers hidden in humans *be used for good."* (Italics added.) And just in case these women (and the free world) didn't get the message, top Soviet biologist Edward Naumov—apparently having received this dictum via ESP—confides in the American authors, "After all, parapsychology is an *international question.* And I believe it's more than just a question of an exchange of research —parapsychology must develop *in the name of good."* (The same bait hooked many an American nuclear physicist and Communist sympathizer into "sharing" atomic secrets so that the atom "could be used for good.")

Need we hear more? The "line" is official—Red-stamped, baited with "good." The Soviet ESP researchers are obviously "the good guys" (that is, the Figure of Sympathy) who are performing their contrived tasks in conformance with the plague technique of the Double Squeeze, with the Moscow Masters as the Figure of Violence.

The March 12, 1974, issue of *The National Enquirer* carried this page-four headline: "RUSSIANS ARE SCARED THEIR PSYCHIC DISCOVERIES WILL BE ABUSED, SAY RESEARCHERS." Written by William Michelfelder, the article begins:

> Russian scientists fear that psychic discoveries involving ESP (extra sensory perception) and mind control will be turned into weapons of war "more deadly than anything the world has known."
>
> The Soviet scientists urgently seek to cooperate with U.S. researchers to prevent the military use of psychic power. . . .

And to insure that no one missed the message of "good will" by the Figures of Sympathy (relayed twice already in the Ostrander-Schroeder book) Edward Naumov, hailed as Russia's "leading parapsychologist," is quoted as saying: "Tell America that psychic discoveries *must be used for the good of mankind*. There is great danger they could be developed as biological weapons more deadly than anything the world has ever known."

And Miss Schroeder adds: "Psychic powers could be used to spread propaganda without people knowing they were being brainwashed."

If these American authors believe the Communist researchers' benevolent intentions in this Double-Squeeze technique, then they indeed have already succumbed to the very threat they present. The Emotional Plague usually *reveals* its intentions, thoroughly and ruthlessly, as in Hitler's *Mein Kampf*, or Khrushchev's boast: "We will bury you!" But the innocence, anxiety, *and refusal to believe in the reality of such evil*, paralyze the intended victim into "cooperation" and, hence, participating in his own destruction.

The emotional-plague technique of the Double Squeeze is about as subtle as a ten-ton truck, and every bit as crushing, if we fail to understand this calculated deceit in time.

The plague "welcomes" us on the one hand, while simultaneously attacking us on the other. Or, the plague attacks on the one hand, then offers pacifying Figures of Sympathy who seek "cooperation for World Peace." (The motive is the same: Get the secrets of the enemy. Learn every trick and gambit in the game of World Power and Human Control. Then spit in his face and shove a cookie into his mouth!)

The emotional plague reveals its real motives by projecting upon the "Enemy" its fabricated fears over the abuse of power. The plague *always* abuses power: human-energy power, nuclear power, gas and oil power; and, if it can, power over minds via ESP. Now the EP word is out for "International cooperation regarding UFOs"!

No truer words were ever written than those by Dr. Elsworth F. Baker, in describing deals between the free world and the emotional plague: "You *cannot* deal with Communists. You will always be betrayed."*

SEX-NEGATION DISGUISED AS "EDUCATION"

Whenever armored man comes into contact with functioning life, he distorts or perverts it. You new Students of the Future will have to be constantly on guard against the Truth-and-Freedom Peddlers who can only twist functional truths into a tangle of grotesque distortions.

In a healthy, sex-affirmative social atmosphere it would not be necessary to *teach* children about sexual matters,

---

*The Journal of Orgonomy, Vol. 5, p. 123. Orgonomic Publications, Inc., Box 565, Ansonia Station, N.Y.C. 10023.

because life-affirmative, genuinely healthy sexual attitudes and genital happiness will be a part of their living experience. But this is still far in man's future—and we shall have to be concerned for many years with the attitudes of armored men and women, and with armored children.

Only the right teacher can develop the healthy educational climate required to discuss the rational sexual needs of children. I said, the "right teacher." The wrong teacher will always kill the living. Sex education in the hands of the wrong teacher is worse than no sex education at all. You must ask yourself: What is the motive for this or that "course" in sex education? And who is teaching it?

You will have to steer the straight and narrow course between sexual anxiety and sexual contempt. If you cannot discuss the pleasure functions of young children without feeling anxious or angry, then don't touch it at all. You cannot fool young children. They will sense your anxiety or contempt; and they will pick up these attitudes from you.

What passes today for "sex education" is really sex *negation.* Passing out textbooks with reproductive organs clearly marked is okay; discussing the birth process is good. But the "hows" and "whys" of such discussions must be clearly revealed and understood. If the teacher is a celibate spinster or nun, if she doesn't have a healthy love-life herself, she can only kill the living. Likewise for the male sadist or homosexual.

Government agencies are making a big fuss over "sexual equality" in schools. You've got to allow girls to participate in formerly all-boys' sports, or government purse strings will be closed. You've got to have the same curfews for girls as boys.

There are colleges today where, it is boasted, students of both sexes sleep in the same dormitories, "and they don't touch each other—they are just like brothers and sisters." *A normal, healthy animal wants to be alone with his mate.*

By encouraging coeducational dormitories, colleges are actually pushing sex-negation. "See, sex is really nothing! Girls and boys sleep together, shower together, and use the same bathrooms. It doesn't mean a thing!" An artificially induced sexual taboo, equivalent to incest, is being inculcated. The loosening of moral restraints on an intellectual level, without first working on the emotional and genital levels, brings contemptuous permissiveness. It is substitute contact, bogus gratification that leads to a dulling and deadening of the sexual functions.

I have worked with many students, armored students, who could not find sexual gratification because of their deep-rooted guilt feelings over sex. So when they are attracted to a mate, the initial attraction is usually replaced by intellectualized negatives: "Ah, she's got freckles on her face and arms; her nose is too small, and she's an ignoramus when it comes to discussing philosophy." In such a manner, the fellow downgrades the girl to justify his fears over touching and loving her. The girls do the same.

Forcing boys and girls to work together, sleep together, play baseball and basketball together, participate in track-and-field meets together—all of this in the name of "sex equality" or "liberation" is pure sham. Girls want to play the so-called boys' games as a substitute for the *real* sexual experiences both sexes crave and require. *First* affirm and protect their God-given rights to love, privacy, and the support of the community in fulfilling their rational sexual needs, and the rest will follow as easily and naturally as the night follows the day.

"Kids today are searching for *their identity*," the sawdust heads of academia are yelling. *To know who you are requires, first of all, that you experience yourself as a sexual animal, that you know in your body the tender streamings and gratification of genital love.* Without such knowing of yourself, you have no roots in Life itself. You can throw all the baseballs and lift all the barbells you like—that still doesn't automatically *make* you anything—neither man, woman nor eunuch! Allowing (*not forcing*) your life, your love-life, to stream pleasurably, to develop pleasurably, to gratify itself pleasurably—these things constitute the roots from which all the other "branches of learning" will grow and develop. And not vice versa!

So beware of the "sex educators" who cannot enjoy genital love, who get their perverted "kicks" out of preaching about "sex education," which, in their hands, becomes a lecture about the horrors of venereal disease or neurasthenia because of masturbatory "excesses." Beware of the educator who leers over his students in the classroom, who pinches his girl students in the name of "sexual freedom," who considers homosexuality "just another liberating sexual experience," who talks like a mechanized robot, without pleasurable emotions, whether he is discussing mathematics or the genital needs of children and young people.

Be very wary of such false and dangerous educators. Learn to read their emotional expressions—in their faces, in the way they use their bodies. Know the tree by its fruit. If possible, observe the *children* of such educators: Are their children warm, open and outgoing, considerate human beings? Or are they bratty, impertinent and sullen creatures? If teachers cannot raise healthy, happy children themselves, what gives them the right to tell you or your children how to live and love?

Education for Life and Love is too important to be entrusted to phonies and sick people. This cannot be stressed too strongly. I hope I've gotten through to you.

THE ABORTION ISSUE

The abortion issue is basically a moral question, and all considerations of morality are, at bottom, considerations of sexual behavior. A rational society based upon the affirmation of natural, primary, God-given heterosexual gratification would have no need to legislate either prostitution or abortion.

Compulsive sexual morality is the spawning ground for all sexual misery. As long as our species cannot gratify primary genital needs in a rational, life-affirmative manner —beginning in childhood and adolescence—we will always have prostitution and abortion, the bad fruit arising from choked and bitter roots.

Every year hundreds of thousands of women, worldwide, have abortions in bathrooms, filthy hovels, or on kitchen tables, at the hands of quacks and other vultures who profit from this traffic in torment. Stopping abortion means prevention, which means a life-positive sex-affirmative education for all children. Such education would include contraceptive education and practical help in obtaining contraceptives. Social protection of the child's and adolescent's Right to Love is also basic to ending this emotional and physical carnage.

Following are excerpts from a letter written by Senator Frank Church which appeared in *Newsweek*, July 14, 1975. Let us look at portions of this letter and then discuss it:

> Freedom of religion embodies not only the common concept that the state should not be controlled by a church, but also the right of individual church members to remain free, in the practice of their religion, from control by the state. If that means that churches cannot, through the utilization of state law prohibit abortion, it must also mean that advocates of abortion cannot use the power of the state to force others to participate in their decision. Consequently the senate approved an amendment of mine that has since become known as the conscience amendment. The legislation prevents the federal government from requiring church-affiliated hospitals and their personnel to perform abortions. . . .
>
> Just because the courts have forbidden states to outlaw abortion does not mean that in a free land we should ever grant the rude demand that some must abort their beliefs by assisting others to abort their babies.

Now, if Man is ever to pull himself out of the deteriorating mess into which he has fallen, he must grow up, and quickly, to the level where he permits only rational expressions and social behavior to have any influence whatsoever on the social scene. In a free society everyone has a right to hold any belief he wishes. But is the opinion of a Wilhelm Reich regarding the cancer process of putrefaction resulting from chronic genital misery (see his *The Cancer Biopathy*) to be equated with the mystical, sex-negative opinions of, say, a Billy Graham? In matters of Love, Work and Knowledge, only those who hold bonafide credentials *in the field under discussion* have the right to be heard on the social scene. The constant warfare of Religion versus Science is the clearest proof of how irrational mysticism has, for centuries, destroyed mankind's greatest benefactors.

Turning to Senator Church's letter: It is clear that Church's response is a *political* one. It is not based upon Truth and Fact, and therefore it is *irrational*. Church's irrational opinion equates scientific knowledge and work with mystical irrationalism and gives them both "equal time." In any form whatsoever, irrational behavior and opinion are the mortal enemies of Life-affirmative work.

In any society, work must of necessity take precedence over any religious belief. (One does not feed, house, and clothe millions by religious litanies and mystical incantations—one must plant, build, harvest, and perform the million-and-one practical jobs required to live.) Where the work itself is rational (i.e., in conformance with fact and truth) and the religious belief or practice conflicts with the work, then the religious belief must not be allowed to confuse or usurp the domain of vitally necessary work! *Work and mere opinion must ever be kept sharply separated!*

We hire firemen to fight fires. Fighting fires is totally rational and totally necessary for the safety and progress of society. Now, if several dozen or several thousand fire-men, because of religious convictions, refuse to fight fires on Sundays, then they must either change their religious beliefs or change their jobs. They cannot have both and do justice to the work.

Similarly, any policeman who refused to kill in the line of duty, because of his religious beliefs, should not be a policeman. It may become necessary (as it often does in police work) to shoot and kill a psychopath or murderous maniac. Religious beliefs against "killing," per se, have no place in such work. Obviously, the same applies to the military.

Abortion is a medical and psychological (emotional) problem dealing with life itself. Only those who know—from a scientific basis—precisely what *LIFE* is all about, how it is created, nurtured and supported, or how it is suffocated, crushed or otherwise destroyed—only such trained and Life-Affirming social specialists have the *factual knowledge* to decide on any specific abortion issue.

Abortion is a personal and private affair between *any woman and her physician.* After all, it is the woman who got pregnant (either with or without her consent), who must bear the new organism, must give it *her* energy, *her* blood and sustenance, and, above all, *her vital energetic contact.* If she doesn't want the child, then she has already renounced the vital contact without which the infant can only become a cripple as well as a future social dependent.

Only those who actually live any problem can best know how to judge it. Celibate priests and nuns, and mystically-oriented medical practitioners and politicians cannot properly judge such a problem—they have no organs for it.

Religion must be kept where it belongs—in the churches. And science must be kept free to do its work in the labora-tories, hospitals, and at the sick beds of the world.

Let us grant then that theology is conversant with the loftiest divine contemplation, and occupies the regal throne among sciences by dignity. But acquiring the highest authority in this way, if she does not descend to the lower and humbler speculations of the subordinate sciences and has no regard for them because they are not concerned with blessedness, then her professors should not arrogate to themselves the authority to decide on controversies in professions which they have neither studied nor practiced.—Galileo*

---

*From *Discoveries and Opinions of Galileo*, trans. by Stillman Drake, Doubleday & Co., N.Y., 1957.

Part Three
Fighting for Life

THE NUCLEAR PESTILENCE

HISTORICAL NOTE

The following material was taken from journals and notes covering a period of several years. It shows the growth and development of the author. Most significant are the connections and interactions between human, emotional events and global and cosmic events. As Reich stated, "Events must be lived to be properly judged."

This narrative is by no means easy to read. It is jumpy, sketchy, often filled with gaps of shorter or longer duration.

The Focus of Attention, however, is always on *Life*, on the functional struggle for personal, human and planetary survival.

May 28, 1957: American A-bomb tests began today. It is amazing to see the change in the students here at Nichols Junior High School, Mount Vernon, N.Y. All show signs of DOR sickness. They have dark areas below their eyes, act "off" and silly, without contact. There has been an upsurge of hitting between boys and girls. (The "antagonzied" external cosmic energy expresses itself biologically in similar antagonistic fashion—in "sharp" behavior, spitefulness, hitting, bullying, etc.) I kept Enid and Steven after school yesterday and sailed into them. I demanded that they stop hitting and teasing each other, disrupting the class. They were much quieter today, avoiding each other.

June 1, 1957: The British exploded another H-bomb on May 30th, three times larger than their previous one. Increase of violence all over the Earth, especially sex crimes among adolescents. Floods in the midwest. An increasing awareness and concern over the fallout problem as evi-

144

denced by news broadcasts and articles—always disclaiming any danger. A report came over Radio Station WOR last night detailing the death of an electronics technician who stood for less than a minute in the path of a radar beam —he was about 10 feet away from its source—and died a few days later. Report stated the man felt "sensations of heat in his stomach."

I know that high-frequency sound waves destroy tissue; high-frequency radio waves may have similar effect.

For the first time since the awards for Teacher of the Year have been made, this year's selection was a *married* woman.

Received a letter from William Steig regarding Wilhelm Reich's imprisonment, March 11th. More money is needed to continue the legal battle. Reduction of sentence was denied. We do not know what to do about this, except help financially however we can.

Wrote a letter to President Eisenhower regarding Dr. Reich's imprisonment, begging him "to free this great and good man." Cried.

June 2, 1957: Awoke about noon. Difficult to get started, DORish. Read Orwell's *Coming Up for Air*, a fine writer, rare—a pity he is dead. References are being made to "Big Brother" (from Orwell's *1984*) in criticism of proposed plans to use television in schools. There is a drive on to get television accepted in schools as a way of alleviating teacher shortages. It would increase spying and automatism, and eliminate spontaneity and the necessary physical (emotional) rapport between teacher and pupil. Unchecked, the present trend toward the use of TV will put them in schools, offices, and homes. A frightening vision.

Gray-black skies all afternoon, blacker about 4 P.M., then thunder-lightning and some heavy rain alleviated the oppressiveness.

Pointed, spiny surfaces are characteristic of DORized organisms—e.g., cacti, scorpions, lizards. The points are probably used or were developed because of the rapid and tremendous need for OR, and *pointed* surfaces draw OR rapidly, e.g., lightning rods. Mesmer would say, the sharp point presents a smaller interstice to the energy and compels it to compress itself—but this is pure mechanism and overlooks the functional processes of a Dorish organism. Interesting to note that automobile designs are becoming more sharp, pointed, spiny.

EXPERIMENT: Shredded and boiled some newspapers yesterday and dropped two bean seeds upon the cooled mass placed in a jar. Used plain soaked, shredded newspaper and two seeds as control. Trying to see if anything will grow on newspaper made highly bionous by boiling.

June 5, 1957: A terrible day. Felt stupid. Couldn't get my bearings at times. Waves of irrational anger. The children looked and acted very tired. Beans on boiled newspaper have germinated. No germination in evidence on controls. U.S. AEC sets off third nuclear bomb in present test, using a balloon! (Note—later this evening, our cat ate my bean plant experiment!)

July 17, 1957: Hottest July 17th in 56 years!! No relief in sight. N.Y. State hit by drought. Floods in Haiti and elsewhere. DOR very bad. DOR-heat in school intolerable. Flu in Korea. (Flu is actually DOR-sickness, i.e., chronic low-level radiation sickness.) Washington weather bureau predicts 30 days of heat. Kansas faces floods. William Sherwood, Stanford Univ. cancer research scientist, killed himself rather than submit to inquiry of UnAmerican Affairs Committee (John Scott's broadcast, WOR, 8:30 P.M.).

July 18, 1957: 96-degree heat yesterday in Mt. Vernon, N.Y. 13% increase in NYC deaths attributed to weather. Ordered a Geiger Counter from Allied Radio, Chicago. *Fourth* atomic-bomb test held this A.M. in Nevada. Desiree and I have decided to hand-set and hand-print Mesmer's *Memoir of 1799.* School is over in three more days. The kids are feeling the DOR. Pornography increasing. Told my social studies students to write out any questions on any subject that they would like me to answer, and if I felt capable of answering them, I would. "*Any* subject?" Yes, any subject. "Can it be *personal?*" Yes, it may be as personal as you wish. Students ranged in age from 13 to 15, boys and girls. Here are some sample questions:

What is your age?
How many children do you have?
Is your wife pretty?
Do you give your children everything they want?
Do you drink liquor? Are you rich?
Who is the first girl you kissed? What age?
Should a boy and girl go steady at age 13?
Should a girl 13 go with a boy 16?
Does hair grow back faster and in greater quantity once it is shaved?
Why does a male attract a female?
What do you see in your wife?
Are you in love with her? Why?
Do you approve of necking?
Do you kiss your wife?
What makes Mr. Eden tick?
Are you attracted to other women besides your wife?
Do you love your students?
Does your wife have a temper like you?
How old were you when you got married?
Should a 14-year-old girl go with a boy 17?
Can you swim?
Do you ever neck with your wife?
Did girls like you when you were young?
How many times a day do you kiss your wife?
What is your religion?
When do you expect to have children? How many?

How much do you weigh? Who buys your clothes?
How long have you been married?
Did you kiss girls when you were 13 or 14?
Why do you ask girls if they have boy friends?
What size belt do you wear?

The preponderance of questions shows a pressing interest in sexuality—the hot-potato subject that is tabooed in schools. I answered all the above questions in as sex-affirmative a manner as I am capable of.

June 28, 1957: Began taking Geiger counter readings in counts per minute (cpms) in our house. Nevada A-test failed to go off! Our cat, Noni, is acting very sluggish, dragging himself around, difficulty in urinating. Board of Education required *third* chest X-ray today. (First time "X-ray machine not working properly"; second time "saw something." I told them I'd had my X-ray dose in the Navy. I asked the X-ray technician if she could tell me what X-ray dosage I was getting each time. *She didn't know!* I asked the same question of the physician. *He didn't know either!* I asked them, "Can you guarantee that your X-rays are doing me no harm?" No answer. I told them I'd taken my last X-ray! They'll have to prove TB, or use a patch test.)

Hurricane Audrey hitting the Northeast. Temperatures dropping. (Note connection between atomic blasts coupled with *strong atmospheric contraction!* When the atmosphere expands violently in one area—atomic-bomb site—it simultaneously contracts in another.)

June 30, 1957: Temperature dropped six degrees in five minutes! I feel strong pressure in diaphragm. Noni (the cat) still sick. Bathed him down with damp wash cloth. Louisiana hit by worst hurricane in 100 years! Hundreds feared dead. Giant explosion on the sun occurred today. Winds to 85 mph in Arkansas.

July 1, 1957: I have severe head pressure and some nausea today. Desiree observed Aurora Borealis around 10

P.M., reaching out with rays of light in the northern sky, north to south. She phoned Hayden Planetarium and Aurora was confirmed.

July 3, 1957: Feathery, pulled DOR clouds. "Largest continental nuclear bomb" set for tomorrow—Fourth of July! Three more solar explosions occurred today. Our DOR-bowl has been filling continuously.

July 4, 1957: Feel a lack of oxygen in the air—stuffy. Earth tremors around Caspian Sea. Thunderstorm at 7 A.M. Two tornadoes in Iowa. "Largest continental A-Blast" detonated in Nevada. Polio outbreak in Tennessee.

July 5, 1957: "Gigantic solar explosion observed by scientists" (WOR Radio, 1 P.M.). What is connection between atomic blasts and solar explosions? I have never believed that our Sun is merely a ball of hot gas, but is an inhabited planet, with a tremendously strong orgone-energy envelope. Is the Sun itself a source of DOR? Twisters and duststorms hit Michigan, Wisconsin, Indiana, Ohio, Minnesota. U.S. Public Health officials en route to Russia in exchange program!

July 6, 1957: Our cat vomited, having difficulty urinating —urine blood-tinged. Europe in throes of 100-plus heat wave. Completed printing of preliminary pages of *Memoir of 1799.* Rooms very active this evening (oranur).

July 7, 1957: Have been taking Geiger counter readings with probe suspended above livingroom floor. Actually count the counts-per-minute, and record for ten minutes. Noticed a *pattern* beginning to show up.

July 10, 1957: Floods in Topeka, Kan. Severe earthquake off Panama; several more quakes in Caspian Sea.

July 12, 1957: Noni still having urinary troubles. More A-bomb tests scheduled. Hate to take Noni to vet—all they know is drugs!

July 13, 1957: Chicago hit by 6 inches rain in 24 hours! Main street under water.

July 15, 1957: Nevada atomic blast went off on schedule

—*seventh* in series! Noni bled all night, took him to vet. Diagnosis, cystitis. Salt Lake City, Utah, records *ten times above "normal" radioactivity!*

July 16, 1957: Sky filled with thin, long cobwebby clouds; DOR-bowl filled during the night. Noni back from vet, antibiotics!

July 18, 1957: Awoke with return of "hay-fever" symptoms, sneezing! Chronic weakness. Have to push to move. Have more energy after sunset on these bad days. (*Note:* When the sun goes down, the atmospheric charge is reduced, and the living organism is better able to discharge energy into the atmosphere.)

July 19, 1957: WAAB Boston reports "critical drought." Massachusetts has hired a cloud seeder! We're drinking much water. Noni seems improved. We still fatigue easily; are using orac (orgone energy accumulator) grounded in fresh bucket of water—*water changed before each use!* Put out water for birds.

July 21, 1957: Hottest day since August 1952. Another A-blast set for this morning.

July 22, 1957: Record heat for date: 97 degrees, despite slight rain.

July 23, 1957: One million acres aflame near Anchorage, Alaska. AEC explodes ninth atomic bomb in series! Connecticut governor asks President to declare entire state a disaster area because of drought. New York and New Jersey hit by drought. $10,000,000 crop loss.

July 25, 1957: Officials ask U.S. Government to designate Rhode Island and Maryland as disaster areas—*drought!*

July 27, 1957: Kiyuchu(?) Japan got *twenty-seven inches of rain in 24 hours!* (Atomic bombs create Oranur, which brings either terrible flooding or drought, JE.) Eleven states in Northeastern U.S. drought-stricken. Noni cries after urinating. Strongest earthquake hits Mexico—100 known dead.

Aug. 2, 1957: U.S. Health authorities warn that "Oriental

Flu" epidemic is expected to hit 1 out of 5 in the U.S., triggered by cold weather. Drug firms preparing serum.

Aug. 4, 1957: We're both feeling very weak. Noni is lifeless. Five new tremors in Mexico City. Torrential rains in Korea. Juvenile violence rampant. New York City Police Force "almost helpless."

Aug. 6, 1957: Noni unable to urinate. Took him to vet who tried catheterization. Bladder burst; Noni died. He was a fine, noble creature. We will miss him. Feel need for orac. AEC explodes eleventh A-bomb.

Aug. 9, 1957: Hurricane Bertha heading toward Galveston, Texas, with winds to 80 mph.

Aug. 11, 1957: Bertha's winds exhausted by the time she hit coast. Heavy rains over most of nation; not enough to break drought. New Jersey Governor Ribicoff says drought loss is at $30,000,000. Delaware River at wading level.

Aug. 15, 1957: "Shasta" Atomic blast postponed 17th time. 25,000 known cases of "Asian Flu" in the U.S. Britain having polio epidemic.

Aug. 18, 1957: "Shasta" A-blast exploded after 19th delay. OR very active. Can't sleep. Great thirst. Got a new cat, "Bobbin."

Aug. 23, 1957: Russia has resumed nuclear testing, exploded large nuclear bomb yesterday. USA sets off 13th nuclear test explosion. I ache all over. Cases of "Asian Flu" spreading throughout U.S. Heaviest cases in New Orleans.

Aug. 26, 1957: Approximately 2 inches of rain fell locally in past 24 hours. Japan scientists suspect Russian atomic test occurred today. U.S. nuclear device "Galileo" exploded this morning. *Sixteenth bomb in this series!* Great Britain to resume nuclear tests this month.

Sept. 4, 1957: School starts today. Completed hand printing of *Memoir of 1799*. A murderous, murky hi-humidity day. "Sky quake" reported over Queens, N.Y., of unknown origin.

Sept. 8, 1957: Atomic bomb exploded this A.M.

Sept. 14, 1957: U.S. explodes 19th atomic bomb in Nevada. News reports 49-year-old man in Hiroshima died of "delayed spinal leukemia" 12 years after U.S. dropped the bomb there.

Sept. 16, 1957: U.S. explodes 20th nuclear bomb from a 1500-foot balloon. Geiger counter cpms sound very erratic. Cigar-shaped UFO seen over London, England.

Sept. 18, 1957: U.S. explodes an "earthquake" atomic bomb 800 feet below earth's surface; 100,000 Americans have "flu." Asian Flu reported on all continents in *ten million estimated cases!*

Sept. 24, 1957: "Whitney" Atomic bomb exploded Sept. 23rd. Russia explodes Atomic bomb. President Eisenhower orders Federal troops into Little Rock, Ark., to quell race riots. (The atomic bombs drive the energy wild in both atmosphere and man.)

Sept. 25, 1957: U.S. atomic test this A.M. Soviets also explode bomb—this time an H Bomb.

Sept. 28, 1957: U.S. explodes its twenty-third atomic bomb! Feel very contracted, sneezing again. Have discovered a significant pattern in my cpms regarding atomic explosions. (This is incomprehensible unless one is aware that the cosmic orgone energy is a continuum, that space is not empty—it is filled with orgone energy.)

Oct. 13, 1957: Between October 8th and 12th Soviets exploded at least two H Bombs in atmosphere—also at least one British Atomic Bomb detected. (*One gets the impression of several criminally minded boys in different street gangs blowing off bombs to impress the "rival gangs" with their potency. Impotent Little Men, criminally insane emotional-plague "scientists" and politicians destroying mankind and their entire planet!*) The head of Dover Press, book publisher, of NYC, attacked Reich and orgonomy over Radio Station WOR, which is heard over 27 states. Connection apparent between EP attack on radio and ad for Martin Gardner's *Fads & Fallacies* in current issue of *Scien-*

tific American. Received notice from Library of Congress that *Memoir of 1799* was selected for the Library's permanent collection.

Oct. 15, 1957: Floods and tornadoes in Texas, flooding in Spain.

Oct. 21, 1957: Flash floods in Haiti. Satellite enters 18th day aloft. Earthquake in Formosa. Pet ram butts Billy Graham. Rains cause havoc in New Mexico. Vermont physician gored by bull.

Oct. 26, 1957: More than 320 dead of "flu" in USA. Earthquake in Tokyo. Typhoon kills nine in Vietnam. Jersey City, N.J., plans to use milk cartons to distribute drinking water. Copies of *Memoir of 1799* sent to Harvard, Columbia Medical Schools, NYU.

Oct. 30, 1957: Orange, N.J., reservoir ran dry! Wells now dry also. Dr. Leroy Burney reports 20,000 "Asian Flu" cases in U.S. (*Note:* 1975—this is DOR-sickness.)

Nov. 1, 1957: Multiple earthquakes reported in Andes Mts.

Nov. 2, 1957: New satellite launched by Russia, circling Earth carrying dog.

Nov. 3, 1957: Awoke with head stuffed; sneezing. Frank McGee of NBC news reported UFO landing on highway on Texas-New Mexico border, stopped a car's engine. WILHELM REICH, M.D., DISCOVERER OF THE LIFE ENERGY, DIES IN LEWISBURG PENITENTIARY. Three-day snowstorm dumps 14 inches of snow in Wyoming. Hartford, Conn., water supply critical. Monsoons in India fail to materialize! Rice crops ruined. U.S. Health Dept. advises second "flu" shots. Radio Moscow claims "new source of power," launched Sputnik II. Earthquake in Israel.

Nov. 4, 1957: "Dazzling object similar to Texas-New Mexico UFO sighted in S. Pacific: cigar-shaped object 200 feet long, 75 feet wide sighted over bunkers at White Sands." Reported by Public Information Officer. Three

Chicago policemen reported a similar sighting. Fiji Isl. clergyman reported UFO "last week."

Nov. 5, 1957: "A New Sound from the Heavens" being reported by ham radio operators on 14.286 megacycles from Alaska to Australia for past 3 days. FCC "can't give out any information—classified." Hams baffled. U.S. Coast Guard cutter reports brilliant UFO sighted south of New Orleans. UFO sighted over Knoxville, Tenn., larger than a jet, "brilliant red-gold hue," oval shape, no wings. Three city firemen saw object coming from Atlanta, Ga. Dr. Lincoln LaPaz, Univ. of Mexico, says, "Nothing interplanetary: either ours or Russia's." Dr. Menzel of Harvard: "Not from outer space." UFO sightings reported again at White Sands, and in Brooklyn, N.Y., by delicatessen owner. U.S.A.F. radar network alerted to watch for "mystery object." R. O. Schmidt (?) of Bakersfield, Calif., reported seeing UFO in Kearney, Neb. A grain purchaser, Schmidt said he saw UFO lying in Platte River dry bed, thought it was a balloon. Approached in his car; car stalled. He got out, walked 30 feet toward object and a light shot out of the craft and paralyzed him. Two men, "in business suits," took him into craft. He said UFO occupants appeared "to be floating inside the craft a few feet above the floor."

Nov. 6, 1957: WOR Radio—UFO knocks out patrolman's radio in car in Urbana, Ill.

Nov. 8, 1957: British explode Hydrogen Bomb in Christmas Isles. Tornado smashes through four Texas Gulf Coast towns. Ten-pound ice chunk drops from sky in Philadelphia, Pa. Six New York City water mains break. Pan American plane lost in Pacific Ocean with 40 aboard. Have written a letter to Father Joseph Lynch of Fordham Univ. Seismic Observatory, outlining my theory regarding cpm-graph patterns and nuclear bomb blasts in atmosphere and under ground. Enclosed copies of my graphs.

Nov. 10, 1957: Rolling earthquake rocked downtown

Tokyo today. Snow flurries this P.M. in Mt. Vernon, N.Y.
Upstate N.Y. gets 15-inch snowfall.

Nov. 13, 1957: Another quake shakes downtown Tokyo.
British plane crashes, 43 dead.

Nov. 24, 1957: Largest sun eruption occurred today—
*largest since 1947. (Check nuclear tests and sun eruptions;
nuclear tests and earthquakes; nuclear tests and "flu" epi-
demics; nuclear tests and crazy, irrational human behavior;
nuclear tests and plane crashes; nuclear tests and UFO
appearances; nuclear tests and infant deaths!)* Sun eruption
will bring magnetic disurbances. *(Also check nuclear tests
and tornadoes and hurricanes; suicides! Worldwide atomic
merchants are emotional-plague characters at their worst!!!)*

Dec. 1, 1957: Quake in Oregon, 11/30; quakes in Toronto
and Chile. Hurricane bearing down upon Oahu, Hawaii.
Strongest quake since 1906 reported in China, *lasting four
hours!* Snowstorms from Maine to Virginia.

Dec. 4, 1957: Earquake in outer Mongolia called "one of
history's greatest" by Soviet scientists: registered 7.6 on a
scale maximum of 8.9.

Dec. 10, 1957: New York City subway strike paralyzes
city. (*Note:* Workers underground are working in "natural
oracus" which increase oranur—i.e., interaction of nuclear
and orgone energy; also metal of subway trains, high-voltage
electricity create intolerable human working conditions, not
to mention fluorescent lights of subway cars.)

Dec. 14, 1957: "Freak killer heat wave hits Japan." Severe
quake kills 1500 in NW Iran. Severe quake in Athens,
Greece. Florida snow-frost destroys crops.

Dec. 20, 1957: Mt. Vernon, N.Y., got 58-degree temperature this P.M., "21 degrees above normal." Tornadoes in
Mid-West. Gale-force winds in NYC. Feel strong pressure
in head. More tremors in Iran.

Dec. 25, 1957: Algiers records 141 tremors in past week!
Australia has 100-degree heat. Typhoon in East China Sea.

Dr. Salk discovers "anti-bodies destroy normal tissue" (AP); Senator Wiley (R. Wisc.) urges U.S. Dept. of Agriculture to study effects of injections of anti-bodies in dairy cattle! (The chemical plague!)

Dec. 29, 1957: Rains finally break worst drought in Sydney, Australia, since 1888. Russia explodes another nuclear blast (12/28).

Jan. 1, 1958: Revolution in Venezuela. (Reich pointed out that, like nuclear-chain reactions, *emotional-chain reactions* occur in the human area.)

Jan. 14, 1958: Volcano on Mana Isl. (New Guinea) erupted for first time in 78 years. Inhabitants evacuated.

Jan. 19, 1958: Several quakes past week: Peru, Austria, Utah. In Borneo, 50,000 face hunger because of rice shortage. Temperature at South Pole hits new high: 5 degrees above zero. Saigon passes law outlawing divorce; 41 die in Lima, Peru, flood.

Jan. 20, 1958: Atomic Energy Commission (AEC) will study radiation in New York City to determine natural background radioactivity. (After so many atom bombs, it is a farce to begin *now* to determine what is "natural"! JE) New Jersey drought continues. "Very severe quake" in Ecuador and Peru. Quake also hits Manila. Japanese note unusually high radioactivity in Central Pacific—7,200 to 10,000 cpms, "may have come from Siberia." Revolt in Caracas.

Jan. 21, 1958: Heaviest snow in 50 years blankets Kansas and Nebraska. Quake in Cuba.

Jan. 22, 1958: Floods in New England. Russia hit by drought.

Jan. 23, 1958: Quake jolts sleepers awake in Taipei, Formosa. Rebels overthrow Jiminez in Venezuela. Gale warning up from Virginia to New York.

Jan. 27, 1958: President Eisenhower's brother died 1/26

of heart attack. Floods in New England. Boston mobilizing
Civil Defense.

Jan. 28, 1958: My students at Nichols Junior High School
reported "eight round orange-colored objects spinning to
the ground behind Nichols Junior High School building—
seen by several students and one parent around 7 P.M.
Juvenile delinquency reported rampant in New York City;
high-school principal commits suicide. Quakes hit midwest.

Feb. 1, 1958: Earthquake in Quito, Ecuador. U.S. satellite "Discoverer" in orbit.

Feb. 9, 1958: Sunspot activity last two days. Eight earthquakes in W. China. Jersey City water main breaks, leaking
1.5 million gallons per hour. Aurora Borealis of great red
intensity stretched to Southwest.

Feb. 17, 1958: Half of U.S. hit by snow and cold. Eight
and one-half inches of snow fell in New York City; 12 inches
in Mt. Vernon. Schools closed; temperature around zero
degrees.

Feb. 23, 1958: Japanese scientists report Russia exploded
H-Bomb, possibly in atmosphere.

Feb. 24, 1958: Russia explodes another H-Bomb in atmosphere, in the megaton range, somewhere in Arctic
Circle.

March 1, 1958: Tornadoes kill nine in Mississippi. Bliz-
zard with 50 mph winds hit Kansas.

March 2, 1958: Bad DOR day here. Geiger-counter graph
patterns show earthquakes plus nuclear bombs.

March 6, 1958: Explorer II "disappeared" after launching—believed "disintegrated."

March 7, 1958: Radioactive cobalt (845 Curies) delivered
to Mid-Eastchester Medical Building on Rt. 22.

March 9, 1958: Earthquake in Taipei.

March 13, 1958: Two jet bombers crash, in Florida and
Oklahoma. Seven inches of snow in Louisville, Kentucky.

Snow in our area, too. Weather Bureau says "lightning and thunder accompanying snow and rain are not unusual." (So why mention it?)

March 14, 1958: Russia explodes two more nuclear bombs today!

March 16, 1958: Strong earthquake north of Tokyo—strong.

March 17, 1958: Second U.S. satellite placed in orbit this A.M.

March 19, 1958: Extremely bad DOR day; DOR clouds sitting on western horizon.

March 21, 1958: New England hit by worst storm in 40 years. Russia explodes two more nuclear weapons.

March 22, 1958: Another nuclear device exploded by Russia.

March 23, 1958: Japan reports radioactivity 200 per cent higher than 1957 level; and 1,000 per cent higher than 1955 level!

March 26, 1958: Satellite No. III aloft today—"bad" orbit.

March 27, 1958: Seventh tremor shakes Virgin Islands since 3/26.

March 29, 1958: Four plane crashes reported. Desiree nauseous for two days.

April 1, 1958: Radioactivity in Denver, Colorado, jumped ten times above normal! Radiation in Scandinavia reported "25% of critical level." Radiation increased in San Francisco. Strong sunspot activity this week.

April 2, 1958: Cyclone hits Brisbane, Australia—blew roofs off 400 houses. Floods in California. Gale winds in New England. Worst weather in northern California in 90 years: 90 mph winds. Tornado in Wichita Falls, Texas. Weather equipment in Soda Springs, Calif., "buried in snow" 80 to 90 inches deep. Golfball-size hailstones in Texas.

April 3, 1958: Strong earthquake 300 miles from Rome, Italy. There were *three* tornadoes yesterday in Wichita Falls, and they were reported as running *counter* to general tornado path.

April 4, 1958: California declared disaster state because of floods. Radioactivity in California rains is twenty-seven times higher than "safe" for drinking water! Scientists believe it is from Soviet tests. Dr. Libby of AEC reports heavy increases of radioactivity in New York area. CBS calls it a "quirk of nature." New York City at same latitude as Siberian and Nevada tests. Northeast part of the U.S. reported as having "highest radioactivity in nation." Dust storms reported in Southwest; floods, tornadoes, etc., noted in many states, also "freak" high tides.

April 5, 1958: The normal background around our house of 20-40 cpms has risen to 50 and 60 cpms (outdoors) with 80 to 90 cpms in some places where rain water stands in puddles. Largest non-nuclear blast of TNT set off today in Canada.

April 6, 1958: Rainfall in San Francisco is 200 times above "normal" in radioactivity; vegetable radioactivity doubled. Capital Airlines Viscount crashed in tri-city airport, Detroit—47 killed.

April 7, 1958: Strong quake 150 miles NW of Hughes, Alaska: 2-hr. duration.

April 8, 1958: Lung cancer rises 3½% in England. Earth's rotation found slowing. Earth shocks in Tokyo, "quite severe."

April 9, 1958: Awoke sneezing. DOR bowls filled! Cpms in water in back of house are 120-200!! Phoned Civil Defense Office, Mt. Vernon, N.Y. Mr. Harry Knox referred me to James Dessey. Gave Dessey cpm readings. He is head of Civil Defense in this area—he didn't know what to do with information. Civil Defense Dept. has no Geiger counters or other monitoring devices of their own!

April 11, 1958: FDA calls drug "Marsalid" (an energizer) "dangerous."

April 13, 1958: Sunny, warm day—no clouds. DOR bowls filling, feel anxious. Jet streams dispersing readily. Two earthquakes in South America. About six USAF plane crashes this week. Tornadoes in Florida.

April 15, 1958: Another series of tornadoes hit Florida. "Remarkable increase in radioactivity" in Switzerland. Dr. Leona Baumgartner, head of NYC Dept. of Health, going to Russia in May.

April 19, 1958: Winston Churchill sick. Former President Hoover's gall bladder removed. I feel weak; chest hurts. U.S. "Thor" missile explodes on launching pad. Navy expects to hit Moon with probe rocket. Tornadoes in Kansas. Man shoots six people in Trenton, N.J.

April 20, 1958: Jet plane crash, Louisville, Ky. Quake offshore California, 60 miles from Berkeley.

April 21, 1958: Plane crash, Nevada desert, 49 dead. "Fireball" seen from West Virginia to South Georgia, showed a brilliant red light.

April 22, 1958: Tornado in Texas; quake in Italy; tornado, South Carolina.

April 23, 1958: Rained buckets last night in our area; many ill with "flu."

April 24, 1958: Rome, Italy, pelted with "radioactive mud."

April 28, 1958: Earthquake off Japan; tornadoes in Mississippi; 2½ inch hailstones, flooding, tornado in Texas. H-Bomb exploded by British—Christmas Island, high altitude. Dr. Linus Pauling finds "Carbon 14 the most deadly radioactive substance from both clean and dirty bombs."

May 2, 1958: Michael Silvert, M.D., associate and co-defendant of Reich, committed suicide. Rain and flooding in Texas all week, violent weather also in Arkansas.

May 7, 1958: Our fifth day of rain. Snow in Blairsville, Ga.

May 8, 1958: Twenty-three inches of rain have fallen in NYC since Jan. 1. Wettest spring in 65 years!

May 11, 1958: U.S. detonates "test explosion," Bikini atoll. My article, "Murder of Animal Magnetism," published in June issue of *Search* magazine.

May 12, 1958: Second U.S. "test" bomb today.

May 16, 1958: Terrible DOR day. Tired. Report of another nuclear test by U.S. today.

May 31, 1958: Tornado warnings—Illinois, Iowa. Quakes recorded in Honolulu, New Hebrides. Tremors felt in San Francisco. Tornado in Kansas. High winds and hail in Missouri, Iowa, Wisconsin, and Illinois.

June 7, 1958: Fordham Univ. seismological center reports moderately strong quake yesterday in Pacific off Mexico. Father Joseph Lynch never acknowledged my letter and cpm graph patterns.

June 8, 1958: Found that salt-water baths are very helpful in overcoming DOR. Eight ounces of salt to tub of luke-warm water, soak for one-half hour, rinse off with fresh-water shower.

June 14, 1958: Terrible DOR day, fog, raw atmosphere. We feel out of contact; "something *big* happened!!! Thunder-lightning last night, three-quarters inch of rain fell here in 30 minutes. "Twisters" reported in New Jersey. Sneezing, weak. TWO TEST EXPLOSIONS TODAY, reported over radio at 11 P.M.

June 16, 1958: Feelings of desperation, severe head pressure and some nausea.

June 17, 1958: Radiation accident injures Oak Ridge, Tennessee, worker.

June 22, 1958: Heavy rains on and off all day yesterday (Oranur rains). Very high charge in house last night—like seeing everything through pools of water.

June 24, 1958: Awoke with headache and anxiety, nause-ous. CPMs indicate another large explosion—unconfirmed as yet.

June 26, 1958: Earthquake pattern developed via cpm graph. Floods in Oklahoma; snow in Colorado and Wyoming. "Freak windstorm" hits New Jersey.

June 27, 1958: Bad DOR, very dry today. Physical weakness continues. U.S. nuclear explosion *confirmed!* Two bombs today exploded within one hour of each other.

June 28, 1958: Tokyo Weather Bureau records nuclear blast (June 29th), tenth of the series. "Strongest atmospheric pressure ever recorded in Japan."

June 30, 1958: Severe DOR emergency appears worsening.

July 1, 1958: Very bad day. High sawtooth graph pattern indicates another bomb. Article on detecting nuclear blasts with Geiger counter sent to Ray Palmer, *Search* magazine.

July 2, 1958: Another scorching day. Twelve-inch rainfall floods Iowa. Two earthquakes, 3 minutes apart in southern Italy. Japan having worst drought in 52 years.

July 4, 1958: Magnetic needles on two of my compasses now pointing south! (What is relationship of Oranur and magnetism?)

July 5, 1958: U.S. explodes twelfth nuclear blast in series.

July 7, 1958: New Jersey Health Commissioner decries X-ray programs as dangerous. A 52-page report has been made under auspices of American Public Health Service.

July 9, 1958: Severe quake in Gulf of Alaska confirms my graph pattern.

July 12, 1958: Tornadoes and 3.9 inches of rain hit Topeka, Kan., yesterday. Emporia winds hit 98 mph. Typhoon Viola swirls north over Iwo Jima.

July 13, 1958: Our pet bluejay is having convulsions. Six minor temblors hit Santa Barbara, Calif.

July 14, 1958: Extremely weak and sleepy. Iraq's pro-U.S. government overthrown. Freak tornado hits Moorestown, N.J. Five thousand U.S. Marines land in Lebanon.

Eight-inch rainfall floods Streeter, Ill. Britain's fleet on standby.

July 25, 1958: Feeling nearly prostrate with weakness. Desiree ill.

July 26, 1958: Desiree continues ill: DOR sickness, very weak. Giving her much fluids and Animal Magnetism.

July 27, 1958: AEC announces fourteenth blast in series (WOR).

Aug. 1, 1958: Fifteenth nuclear explosion announced! Detonated 110 miles in space over Johnson Island—seen in Hawaii, 700 miles away. Floods in Missouri.

Aug. 2, 1958: No energy.

Aug. 5, 1958: Can't seem to fight off chronic weakness.

Aug. 6, 1958: DOR worsens, like a tightening of a screw, a turn a day. Our new kitten acting very nervous. We feel extremely distressed.

Aug. 8, 1958: Japan reports that sailors on the *Kaskawa Maru* were sprayed with radioactive material 400 miles from "danger zone" of current tests. Last month, American seamen from two oceanographic ships were treated in American hospitals! Weakness continues; work in spurts, muscles ache.

Aug. 9, 1958: United Nations calls for end to atomic tests. AEC says "man must learn to live with radiation."!!!!!

Aug. 10, 1958: "Freak" hurricane-like winds (to 46 mph) kill one in Poughkeepsie, N.Y.; hit New York City and Westchester.

Aug. 11, 1958: Nuclear explosion—another one.

Aug. 12, 1958: DOR chronic, weakness continues.

Aug. 15, 1958: Hurricane Cleo off Florida. Cpms sound very weak. Two severe quakes reported, one near Philippines; other near Soviet Siberia. KLM plane crash kills 99. (Pilots get DORized too; get out of contact.) Twenty-three die in airliner crash in Nantucket.

Aug. 16, 1958: Two quakes today—Philippines and near Japan.

Aug. 17, 1958: U.S. rocket to the moon explodes after 77 seconds. *Six major plane crashes in past seven days,* killing 213 people. Four days of earthquakes in Iran! Fire consumes 1200 acres in Montana Glacier National Park. Another Japanese victim of World II atom bomb, died today.

Aug. 18, 1958: We both felt deep melancholy.

Aug. 19, 1958: Iran earthquakes continue. "The orgone box" ridiculed by Dorothy Kilgallen over WOR radio this A.M. Goes to 27 states.

Aug. 21, 1958: A very bad "lost" day, smaze, weakness. Can't work.

Aug. 22, 1958: Britain explodes nuclear bomb from balloon over the Pacific. Feeling very anxious, distressed. Satellite V fails to orbit.

Aug. 23, 1958: Worst floods in history hit Austria. Sleeping sickness epidemic in Japan and Korea. Sent an article, "Emotional Plague *versus* Animal Magnetism," to *Orgonomic Medicine.* (It was later returned: "Not enough suitable material.")

Aug. 24, 1958: A dirty-gray DOR day. Can't get moving.

Aug. 25, 1958: Hard rain, thunder all day. Communists shell Quemoy Islands for fourth day—500 dead. Tremendous explosion rocks Marseilles fuel depot, 20 firemen killed. Hurricane Daisy off Florida. Typhoon hits Japan.

Aug. 26, 1958: Largest mining blast detonated in Minnesota.

Aug. 27, 1958: Giant magnetic storm on the sun!

Aug. 29, 1958: Hurricane Daisy veered off New England Coast—forecasters are "red faced." (CORE operations?) AEC reports that ten "small" nuclear devices will be exploded in Nevada in next two months. Race riots in Britain for fourth straight day.

Sept. 2, 1958: Great Britain explodes H-Bomb.

Sept. 3, 1958: I was severely contracted last night—went through severe cold symptoms in matter of hours; used orac repeatedly.

Sept. 4, 1958: Static (energy discharge) on radio. Hurricane Ella 400 miles off Mississippi. Rain and hailstorms hit Great Britain: "Severest in London's history."

Sept. 6, 1958: High humidity. "Smog" over Mt. Vernon, N.Y., air clammy and putrid.

Sept. 9, 1958: Contracted again with another "cold." Using orac repeatedly.

Sept. 12, 1958: Odd-looking clouds coming over. Desiree not feeling well.

Sept. 16, 1958: Graph patterns indicate underground nuclear blast.

Sept. 19, 1958: AEC begins last ten nuclear bombs in new series. One today.

Sept. 20, 1958: Another bomb today.

Sept. 21, 1958: Ten inches of rain falls in last few hours in Orange, Texas! Floods, twisters also reported.

Sept. 23, 1958: Severe earthquake in Iran.

Sept. 30, 1958: Two Russian nuclear explosions.

Oct. 2, 1958: Two more Russian nuclear explosions.

Oct. 5, 1958: Subjective feelings of severe distress and anxiety. Have completed writing the last chapter to *Suffer the Children* and sent it to printer.

Oct. 7, 1958: Very bad day again. Felt light-headed. USSR resumed testing. Approximately five nuclear bombs exploded this past week (between USA and USSR). Russia exploded her sixth bomb since Sept. 20th; U.S.A. blew off her fourth in Nevada in current series. "Spider webs" (associated with UFOs) fell all over Portales, New Mexico. Huge cigar-shaped UFO sighted over San Andreas Mountains near Alamogordo, N.M., reported by Frank Edwards.

Oct. 12, 1958: Russia sets off seventh in series.

Oct. 14, 1958: DOR clouds coming over from southwest

to northeast, in armies. Both of us ill at work: weak, headache, nauseous.

Oct. 15, 1958: Russia detonates "large" thermonuclear bomb today—eighth in series. U.S. detonates two today: one in a tower; one underground, "large."

Oct. 18, 1958: Another "sizable" nuclear bomb by Russia; and another by the U.S. USAF fighter plane explodes, aircraft's wings found near Monmouth, N.J. Heavy rains in New Mexico, Rio Grande River rampaging.

Oct. 19, 1958: Russia explodes tenth nuclear bomb since Sept. 30th. A terrible day. Two more bombs exploded by U.S.

Oct. 20, 1958: Russia blows off eleventh bomb today—"relatively large."

Oct. 22, 1958: Russia explodes twelfth nuclear bomb. U.S. blasts three more!

Oct. 23, 1958: Rain here all day.

Oct. 24, 1958: Russia explodes thirteenth bomb—high in atmosphere.

Oct. 25, 1958: Russia explodes fourteenth bomb: "large."

Oct. 26, 1958: U.S. detonates two nuclear bombs today (another expected)—this makes ONE HUNDRED AND TWENTY-FIVE NUCLEAR DEVICES DETONATED BY THE U.S.A. thus far!

Oct. 27, 1958: Another U.S. bomb.

Oct. 30, 1958: Two U.S. nuclear bombs exploded today. John Wingate, news broadcast over WOR radio: "Los Angeles city officials protesting radioactivity of more than 1,000 cpms."

Nov. 1, 1958: New York City has record 46-inches of rain thus far in 1958, with two months still to go.

Nov. 3, 1958: One year after Reich's death. Very BAD day. Cpms 110 outdoors in rain puddles.

Nov. 4, 1958: Feeling absolutely miserable. DOR clouds

all day. Using orac repeatedly with draw tubes into fresh-water bucket. Just learned that Russia exploded another two nuclear bombs: Nov. 1 and Nov. 3.

Nov. 7, 1958: Earthquake felt in Illinois, Indiana, Missouri, Kentucky. People seem to be "cracking." Temperature here has risen in the 60's! Atmosphere very DORish.

Nov. 18, 1958: Four days of solid DOR. No relief. Whenever we think, "It can't possibly get worse"—*IT DOES!*

Dec. 31, 1958: Plague attack on Reich: "Long John" Radio Show (WOR).

Part Four
The Mount Vernon Affair

HISTORICAL BACKGROUND

What follows is the first historical account of the emotional plague *versus* functional education in the United States. For the first time in American education, a functional educator openly *affirmed* the rational, primary sexual needs and expressions of his students in a public school. Jerome Eden took upon himself the responsibility for answering the pressing sexual questions of his adolescent students in junior and senior high schools in 1952 and 1953. The questions of his students were published by Reich in the June 1955 issue of *Orgonomic Medicine*, in the article, "Adolescent Genital Misery."

In 1956, Eden began working as a teacher in Nichols Junior High School, Mount Vernon, N.Y., under Dr. George Cohen, principal. His knowledge of orgonomy, his own restructuralization, and his long contact with children and young people in summer camps (where he had been a program director) in the U.S. Navy, and in education, convinced him of the truth of Reich's formulations regarding the primacy of sexual energy as the motivating force of human life. In every educational situation, Eden saw with his own eyes and felt with his own body the disastrous effects of frustrated sexual energy in his students. Students took to him immediately, for they felt his deep concern and contact. And because he was able to work with the most "unmanageable" students, he was usually given the more difficult disciplinary classes, which invariably won each term's award for best attendance. His students came to his classes, not out of any compulsion, but because it was pleasurable to do so.

Inevitably, as each new crop of students came to trust

Eden as a friend, sexual questions would arise spontaneously. It usually took months of hard work, however, before the proper educational climate had been established which could allow for such expressions to surface openly. And whenever the rational, heterosexual needs of the students were affirmed and approved, *the school work would likewise improve!*

It was therefore not a matter of "teaching sex" to students, but of permitting the proper sex-affirmative climate to develop naturally in the classroom. Nevertheless, there were several dangers involved. First were the emotional-plague people, who always "smell out" the presence of Life in any situation. Second were the highly armored educators themselves, who cannot tolerate the highly-charged expressions of youngsters, and prefer, as Reich called it, "the drill-and-squeeze" methods of authoritarian education. And third are the students themselves, who are torn between knowing the truth behind sex-affirmation while, at the same time, suffering from the anxiety and guilt of their own armoring.

Critics have questioned the wisdom of attempting to affirm natural genitality in a public-school situation. They claim it can only lead to trouble; and it did. It cost Eden and his wife deep emotional wounds, and the loss of his career as a teacher. Eden dangerously misjudged the virulence of the emotional plague in education. He acted out of his deep contact with Life and his willingness to "go all the way" to help that Life. His inexperience brought him to the brink of disaster. It is, however, always easier to criticize than it is to roll up one's sleeves and try to clean up the mess of sexual misery; and theoretical knowledge is a sham if it cannot be put into practical effect.

Now let us follow the events as they took place in 1959 and later. It is hoped that what follows will aid Students of the Future in their battle to Fight for Life and Focus on the Essential.

January 1, 1959: The old year went out with a bang.

Jack Green, editor and publisher of "Newspaper," was interviewed on the "Long John" radio show (WOR, N.Y.C.). He said Wilhelm Reich was mentally ill the last two or three years of his life. I wrote him, telling him to keep his crap to himself, and canceled my subscription.

I sent out 67 notices regarding my proposed orgonomic publication *FORE* (For Orgonomic Education); only three subscribers: Lack of interest or fear to become associated with orgonomy so soon after Red Fascist attack and FDA injunction. So we have decided to let *FORE* die in inception. *First* should come the *need*, then the fulfillment; not vice versa. William Steig suggested returning to private work, such as publishing The Eden Press books. He is right —a very fine person.

Suffer the Children is now being made into page proofs. Very little social life. Just our cat, our blue jay, "Casey," and "Zippo" the turtle. And our work. There is no substitute for good, rational work. I look forward uneasily to going back to teaching after this restful, workful Christmas vacation, though the atmosphere remains very DORish. Last week, NYC reported 25% increase in radioactivity! God help us.

Jan. 13, 1959: I was called by Dr. Cohen to report to his office this morning during my free period. He told me that several parents had complained to him about my teaching activities. I asked him who the parents were, but he refused to name them. He said his chief complaint was that I had substituted the *Diary of Anne Frank* for *Treasure Island*, and that the *Diary of Anne Frank* was not a part of the curriculum. I told him that my students in one all-girl class had asked for the substitution and had voted 28 to 2 to read the *Diary*. He said he'd heard it was *a pornographic book*, although he had not read it himself. My reply was that the book was a classic, much more meaningful for adolescent girls than *Treasure Island*, and that Mrs. Eleanor

Roosevelt would hardly write the "Introduction" to a pornographic book. That didn't matter—I was to reinstitute the reading of *Treasure Island.*

(In recalling these events, I remember that last term my class had put on a school play for the student body entitled "You Can't Take It With You." While rehearsing the play late one afternoon in the auditorium, the students laughed uproariously over one of the many comic incidents they were rehearsing. Dr. Cohen happened to be passing by the open doors to the auditorium and heard the laughter. The following morning he stopped me and inquired whether the play we were rehearsing *was pornographic!* It is extremely significant to note what passes through the minds of armored educators.)

Jan. 14, 1959: Dr. Cohen again called me into his office to answer the following complaints:

Parents were objecting to my anti-Communist discussions in my social studies classes, and my use of J. Edgar Hoover's *Masters of Deceit.*

Parents were objecting to my discussions of sexuality in my classrooms.

Parents were objecting to my discussions of UFOs with my students.

I informed Dr. Cohen that I believed in permitting my students the democratic freedom to discuss or write about any subjects which interested them. I said I felt it was very important that they understand the true nature of Red Fascism.

As for UFOs, I reminded Dr. Cohen that it was a subject of deep interest to my students, that I had lectured on the subject before the school's Aviation Club (at the club's request) and had studied it for many years.

As for discussions of sexuality, I said that it was apparently of vital importance to young people, that they had repeatedly asked me questions which they could not or would not ask anyone else, and that I felt it my duty to respond to their needs in a responsible manner.

Dr. Cohen then made a formal request that I refrain from discussing with my students any of the following topics: Communism, sexuality, or UFOs. He asked me if I thought such a request was "arbitrary, dictatorial and a restriction of academic freedom." I said yes.

Dr. Cohen's manner was very civil and unemotional. His apparent concern was strictly "academic." The subjects I was discussing were "not proper subjects" for my classes. I was exercising "poor judgment" in pursuing them. I left his office and returned to my classes—nothing had been settled, but I knew this would not be the end of the matter.

I later realized that Miss Mary Reynolds, assistant principal and school counselor, was the emotional-plague character. It was Miss Reynolds who had stopped one of my students in the hall and confiscated the girl's copy of the *Diary of Anne Frank*, telling the girl she was going to call the girl's mother "to check to see if she had permission" to read such a book! I went to Reynold's office and demanded the return of the book. She told me she'd heard that "the book is pornographic, and not fit reading for adolescent girls." She said she'd never read the book.

Other students told me that Mary Reynolds cornered them and was always inquiring about "what is going on in Mr. Eden's classes?" I told Miss Reynolds that if she wanted to know what was going on in my classes, all she had to do was ask me. I got the book back and returned it to the student who was, incidentally, extremely upset and close to tears.

Feb. 13, 1959: This was the day! Dr. Cohen called me into his office. Either I stop discussing sexuality with my students or I will not receive tenure. (I lacked six months toward full tenure at this time.) I refused.

Dr. Cohen said: *"I would have lost all respect for you had you reacted otherwise!"* (The emotional plague admires as it destroys.) I am charged by him with using "poor judgment." I will not receive tenure. Dr. Cohen then told me to return to my class. I did so, advising each class in turn that I didn't think I would be with them much longer. And I told my students *why* I would not be allowed to teach them. Many wept. There was talk of a student strike and petitions. I advised them not to do anything rash, but never to forget what had happened: "What the majority wants they will get."

Later in the day, Dr. Cohen sent a note to me to wait for him in the teachers' lounge—a substitute would take the remainder of my classes. I went to the lounge, locked myself in the men's room and vented some of the agony. No one else was in the lounge, and I was grateful for the solitude.

About an hour later, Dr. Cohen entered the lounge and said that he had phoned Miss Catharine Rhodes, assistant superintendent of schools. She had told him to advise me "to resign, effective immediately." I said I would not resign.

If I resigned, Dr. Cohen said, he would give me a letter of recommendation so that I might teach in another school system. But if I did not resign, then no letter would be given.

I said again that I would not resign, that I was guilty of no crime, that I always taught with the interests of all of my students in mind, and that if I were a bad teacher in Mount Vernon, then I did not deserve to teach anywhere else.

Dr. Cohen said that I was to see Miss Rhodes at 3 P.M. that afternoon.

As I had no money for taxi fare, I walked across town to the Board of Education Building. Miss Rhodes saw me immediately. She had a letter of resignation already prepared on her desk for me to sign. Would I sign it? No. She had acted as prosecutor, judge and jury. Did I know that there was a Board of Education ruling which prohibited the teaching of sex in Mount Vernon schools? I did not.

She gave me the impression of a "very sympathetic" academician—"concerned with *my* welfare!" Actually, what was desired was to end the matter immediately, so that there would be no fuss, no publicity, no stink. The Superintendent of Schools, Dr. Jordan Larson, was at a convention in Atlantic City, N.J., and would not return until February 19th.

Miss Rhodes said that the best thing was to "remove the victim" (meaning me), and that I was not to return to my school until notified to report for a hearing before Dr. Larson. She "guaranteed" that I would be present to answer charges against me.

I walked back across town to my home as one who has just heard the sentence of death pronounced. Suddenly, I found myself praying soundlessly—for myself, my wife, the students. *"How far, dear God, must I go?"* I found myself on the corner of an intersection in the business district. Across the street in a store-front was a huge sign in large red letters on a white background. The sign read: *"Everything must go!"* I suddenly felt very calm and at peace.

At 6 P.M., William Cullen of the National Education Association phoned to say he had heard about my situation. (Such news travels like wildfire.) When I told him of my tenure status (that is, that I lacked 6 months to full tenure) he said I had no legal leg to stand on. He suggested I start looking for another job.

Later, students began coming to my home; they wanted me to tell them what they should do. I said I couldn't tell them what they should do—it was up to each person to do what he thought best.

The following morning (Feb. 14, 1959), Dr. George

Cohen telephoned and asked me to reconsider my refusal to resign. I told him I would never resign. He asked to speak to my wife. I hung up on him.

My wife was very upset, fearing that the plague would accuse me of "immoral" acts in an attempt to destroy me as Homer Lane, the great British educator, had been destroyed.

Parents of my students began phoning, asking if my dismissal were true; wanting to know what could be done. I assumed there would be a hearing with a chance to face my hitherto anonymous complainants, and I suggested that those who wished to do so should try to attend the upcoming hearing. The phone rang every few minutes until late in the evening when I began writing, "Poor Judgment—a Functional Educator's Response." I wrote steadily until early morning, trying to clarify the real issues at stake which boiled down to the Child's Right to a Healthy Love Life.

In this pamphlet I asserted that I would attend any hearing provided: (1) That I were furnished with a list of specific charges; and (2) that I be given an opportunity to question any complainants, face to face. I categorically refused to respond to anonymous complaints. This, I maintained, was the basic right of any citizen and responsible worker.

The pamphlet also discussed the following points: In a democratic society, educators have the duty to *educate* in a democratic fashion. Democracy cannot be taught—it must be lived. Therefore, allowing my students to discuss or write papers on topics which interested them was simply allowing them to experience democracy in their daily lives.

I publicly affirmed the fact that I had discussed sexual problems which my students had brought up, adding that "If Life cannot love, it can only hate." I called attention to the growing social mess called "juvenile delinquency," a direct result of genital frustration in young people.

I further publicly affirmed that I had felt it my duty to expose my students to the organized emotional plague of Red Fascism (Communism) and that, for my text, I had used J. Edgar Hoover's *Masters of Deceit.* I added that had I spoken out *for* Communism it would have been far safer for me and my career. (Undoubtedly many liberal and left-ist-leaning organizations lost any sympathy for me in view of such a "reactionary" stand.)

As for UFOs (Unidentified Flying Objects) and the anonymously-motivated charge that I was "unnecessarily frightening my students," I mentioned that I had been invited to speak on the subject by the school's Aviation Club; that students had voiced a burning interest in the subject, that various government agencies were likewise intensely concerned, and that the only ones frightened by discussions of UFOs were certain anonymous parents as well as educational administrators.

On February 17th, Ruth Weber, reporter for the Mount Vernon *Daily Argus,* phoned me and asked if she could interview me that night. We met, and I told her what happened. She listened with good contact, and said, "My God, what are they going to do with you?"

I said that true justice in this case would require Dr. Cohen's immediate resignation; and, if the world were rational, I should replace him as principal. She thought I was joking; but I was deadly serious.

The next day I had 1,000 4-page pamphlets of "Poor Judgment" from the printer, and began mailing them out to the 400 school teachers in the Mount Vernon system, to the administrators, to the press. Since my terminal paycheck was still pending, we had very little money left. In the evening I got a phone call from a representative of National Citizens Committee for Public Schools. He just wanted me to know that such a committee existed to help fight for better schools and "good teaching conditions." There was no offer of help to fight for me, however.

My own personal position had clarified into the following: If I was given a fair, unbiased hearing as outlined in "Poor Judgment," I would attend any review of my "case." I wrote a letter to that effect to Superintendent of Schools, Dr. Jordan Larson, P.O. Registered No. 10820, receiving the return receipt on February 18, 1959. A copy of the letter was sent to Ruth Weber of the *Daily Argus*.

On February 19, 1959, the following front-page article appeared in the *Argus*:

Prejudged, He Asserts
Won't Attend "Review"
Of Case, Teacher Says

Jerome Eden, Nichols Junior High School teacher who has become a storm center in a controversy over his "teaching procedure," disclosed today that a school official had asked for his resignation Friday, that he had declined to give it and that he had then been suspended.

The suspension was imposed, he said, by Miss Catharine Rhodes, assistant superintendent, pending a "review" of his case by Superintendent Jordan L. Larson.

In a letter sent to Dr. Larson, Mr. Eden asserted that he "cannot consider" appearing at such a review because he feels that "the issues involved have already been prejudged" against him, and because the charges made by Dr. George Cohen, Nichols principal, "developed out of a series of malefide complaints by parents who refused to confront me or be identified." Mr. Eden adds that Dr. Cohen told him that he had promised the complaining parents not to disclose their identities.

In expanding his reasons for not being willing to appear at a "review" of his case, Mr. Eden says that *minimum conditions under which he could agree to attend would be that he receive a full and complete written statement of the charges, with sufficient time to review them; that he be allowed to confront and examine his accusers; and that he be permitted to present such material, witnesses and testimony as he felt necessary.*

Mr. Eden, whose suspension resulted in a reaction strongly in his favor among some students, disclosed in a written reply sent to Dr. Larson and the press that Dr. Cohen held that he, Mr. Eden, had "exercised poor judgment in discussing with my students certain topics which Dr. Cohen felt were either improper or beyond the scope of 8th and 9th grade students."

Among these topics, according to Mr. Eden's statement, were the problems of adolescent sexuality, flying saucers, and communism and the threat it poses to the democratic way of life. Dr. Larson, who has been attending school administrators' meetings in Atlantic City, is expected to return to Mount Vernon today. (Above italics supplied, JE)

This was the second page-one story about the case to appear in the *Daily Argus*. The first had appeared on February 18, 1959, headlined:

Students Defend Him
PARENTS' COMPLAINTS BAR
TEACHER FROM CLASSES

Ruth Weber of the *Argus* treated the facts fairly and objectively, and I was grateful to her.

February 20, 1959—Some Notes: There seems to be some significance to the fact that *assistants* in high positions of trust are the ones to watch. In a private school it was the assistant to the principal who was the emotional-plague character. In Nichols, it was the assistant to the principal (Mary Reynolds) who was the sniper and match-thrower, with her vicious gossip, undermining and evident hatred for me. In the Board of Education, again the assistant to the Superintendent of Schools asked for my immediate resignation—without a hearing.

Mistakes of JE in this Case: (1) JE should never have left his classroom until formally notified of his suspension. He did this out of his own anxiety—after two and a half years of harassment and sniping which had worn him down. One cannot fight the plague with daily contact and not become infected! (2) JE actually *thanked* Catharine Rhodes for "being fair"!!! He should have required, then and there, a formal, *written* Statement of Charges, properly signed, showing exactly who was accusing him of what. The first thing Miss Rhodes had said to JE was, "I hear you've gotten yourself into *some* problem." She wanted him to explain (*confess*) before proceeding with the interview. (Brainwashing technique of the emotional plague which *knows* that all human beings are "guilty" of something.)

JE was taken completely in by her "sympathy" and apparent "understanding" attitude. He should have demanded to know why she had prejudged him! He did ask what she had heard before speaking. Her first topic was that he had been talking about Flying Saucers from outer space which had some "unknown powers." (It is very evident that *someone* was continuously monitoring JE's classes, pumping his students, spying in the typical manner of the emotional pestilence.) The fact that Miss Rhodes had the suspension letter all ready upon his arrival attests to the total lack of any bonafide, responsible attitude on her part.

A major point was completely overlooked in the "Poor Judgment" pamphlet: A decent and responsible educator should never be harassed and persecuted for his educational opinions. (*Note*—1974, *providing* they are sufficiently supported by verifiable evidence!)

In a democratic society, functional educators, fighting for the *New Generations*, must not ever be forced to face charges which are malicious, or which stem from pathological snipers (be they parents, priests, etc.) whose very complaints demonstrate a complete lack of interest in the *welfare of the Child*. (*Note:* Right here, JE is beginning to *experience* what Reich went through with respect to harassment and persecution by the FDA and political hoodlums. One tries to do one's job—be he educator, carpenter, or research scientist—and finds his work, his life, his hopes a chaos because of irrational, neurotic behavior.)

A Functional Educator who is the bulwark of Democracy, and whose major and sole primary responsibility is to see to it that his children have every opportunity and the emotional climate consistent with *their* needs (primary needs), should never be forced to answer malefide complaints motivated by jealousy, hatred for the child, or commercial or pathological interests.

The fact that a person is a parent in the "legal" sense does not mean that *ipso facto* he or she is a parent in the moral or Natural-Lawful sense. Society must look consistently at the Child, at the Child's needs and whether or not they are being met. Too many parents for too many years have been crippling and killing children under protection of legalities and formal technicalities which protect and support such evil.

February 21, 1959: I walk through town and parents of my students stop me with tears in their eyes and say what a shame the whole thing is, and what can they do. I tell them they will have to fight for what they want, that *two* parents objected to the *Diary of Anne Frank*, while twenty-eight remained silent, thus—*two became the majority!* For the most part, the parents cannot fight, they are afraid to "make waves," to stick their necks out, to get involved in a rational fight for Life.

I had to call in a physician this afternoon to attend to Desiree. She was contracting severely with fear and worry. The physician, a Yonkers resident, prescribed a sedative. He had known about the case and was very sympathetic. He refused to charge me a fee when I told him that I had no funds and was still awaiting my terminal paycheck. Dr Elsworth F. Baker sent a message via a friend: "Do not underestimate your opponent." I will try to remember that advice.

February 22, 1959: Have been getting severe anxiety attacks myself, with shortness of breath and pains in the chest at night in bed; feelings of acute need for air. Worked on my armor. Students came to the house to inform me that they had petitions with hundreds of students' names which they will take to the Board of Education. It is gratifying. But who listens to children?

NOTE: Dr. Jordan L. Larson gave out a statement to the press which stated that I had indeed exercised "poor judgment" and had exhibited "disdain over parental objections to my teaching methods."

Thus, Dr. Larson too prejudges the issues! And I was supposed to get a "fair hearing"?

February 23, 1959: Bobbin our new kitten is very weak, won't drink or eat anything. Breath fetid.

February 24, 1959: Received a letter from Dr. Larson giving me the opportunity to meet him for a conference. "Only the formalities count," said Reich. After Cohen prejudges me, after Catharine Rhodes prejudges, and now Larson prejudges me, they want "to confer" with me. Cartoon on editorial page of *Argus* depicts rampant juvenile delinquency with a caption: "Someone Is Falling Down," with accompanying editorial concerning the 2,000,000 juvenile delinquents in the United States and the inability of schools, churches, homes, police or courts to cope with the situation.[*]

Thirty-one of my students have thus far come to visit me. But not a single one of my "fellow educators" has as much as phoned. *Don't touch it!*

Feb. 25, 1959: Received a postcard from a teacher in New Rochelle, N.Y. He says he too has received "anonymous complaints" from parents. He will be "watching the case with interest." Don't *fight,* Buster! Just "watch with interest!" And you'll be next!

---

[*]The situation worsens without letup until today "education" is totally chaotic. JE, 1976.

Took our kitten to the vet. He was put "to sleep," by injection. At least armored man can kill painlessly.

Feb. 26, 1959: The New York Times:

PILOT REPORTS SAUCERS
Says Airline Passengers and
Crew Saw Lights

DETROIT, Feb. 25 (AP)—The pilot of an American Airlines DC-6 passenger plane said today that three mysterious objects that looked like shining saucers appeared to accompany the plane for forty-five minutes last night on its nonstop flight from Newark, N.J., to Detroit.

Capt. Peter Killian of Syosset, L.I., said other members of the crew and thirty-five passengers also saw the flying objects. The plane left Newark at 7:10 P.M. . . .

Captain Killian said he radioed two other American Airlines planes flying in the vicinity. . . . He said both other captains radioed back that they had seen the flying objects too.

Received a letter today from Dave Knickerbocker, feature writer for the *New York World Telegram and Sun,* asking for a copy of my pamphlet "Poor Judgment." He said he had gotten a news release from the Board of Education on my case and wanted to hear my side of the story. The plague fears "exposure." It thinks I must be sending my pamphlets all over the place, when all I've done is send them to teachers and others here, locally. Sent Knickerbocker a pamphlet. (And never heard from him again.)

NOTE: Dr. Larson was quoted (Feb. 20, 1959) in the *Argus* in the following exchange:

Asked if he will see Mr. Eden, he replied, "I am not sure, in the light of his expressed refusal to appear before me for any review of the matter."

This is a lie. I told Dr. Larson that I would indeed appear for a review, provided he would give me a just and impartial hearing. I stipulated my conditions in my pamphlet "Poor Judgment." I asked for formal charges; an opportunity to prepare a proper defense; and a chance to confront and examine my accusers. That is no more than any common thief is given in a court of law. It is simple *due process.* I stipulated these conditions again to Dr. Larson in a personal letter, as already noted, sent via registered mail—which he received.

According to the *Argus* story of Feb. 20, 1959, here is how Dr. Larson reveals himself:

> Asked if, from the material he has seen so far, he believes Mr. Eden has acted in a manner unbecoming to a teacher, Dr. Larson said, "From the information that has come to me, there is ample evidence of poor judgment on the part of this teacher and impropriety of conduct both as to extraneous subject matter discussed, as to substituting his own choice of books for those in the approved course of study, and as to refusal to accept instructions from his principal to make changes in his procedures in this regard."

(*Note:* Whether it is "proper" or "improper" to discuss the problems of adolescent genitality in a classroom is today not even debatable. There are now State and Federally-sponsored courses on "sex education." The crucial matter is, of course, not "sex education" per se; but *who* will teach it; and *how* will the genital needs of youth be handled—in a healthy affirmative, or perverse and negative manner!)

The second issue, the substitution of *books* (there was only *one* substitution, the *Diary of Anne Frank* for *Treasure Island*), Dr. Larson fails to mention that I *agreed* after a directive from Dr. Cohen, to use *Treasure Island.* My "refusal to accept instructions" from my principal means I would not refrain from my responsibilities of dealing with the *whole* child (genitals as well as brains!); that if my students were undernourished, I would feed them first; that if they had splinters in their feet, I would first remove the splinters; and that while they are suffering agonies based on chronic sexual stagnation, it is insanity to "teach *Treasure*

Island." A functional educator deals with *first things first!*

These statements by Dr. Larson clearly reveal his own prejudice. I will not now attend any so-called "hearing" designed to publicly rubber-stamp a decision which has been privately agreed to.

What contempt for work! No one asks *the children* about me. The carpenter is judged by his work; the bricklayer by his building. *But no one goes to my children!* And who will "judge" the issues? A Board of Education! Made up of whom? Anthony Scarpino, James W. Thornton, a dentist; Ruth G. deLemos; James F. Gallagher; August P. Petrillo; Frank E. Pierce; Morton Sultzer; Arthur Taft; John J. Yannantuono. Not a single member of the Board of Education is my "peer"! Not a single one is an educator. Imagine running the Federal Aviation Agency with a board comprised of plumbers; or the AMA by a board of directors comprised of woodcutters! These non-educators are to sit in judgment of *my work*, empowered to do so by "the people."

Once again fruitful, factual work is left to the mercy of chance. Truth will be crushed by personal opinion and prejudice. God help this town!

March 2, 1959: Suffer the Children arrived this morning from the printer. A very nice job. Phoned the printer and complimented him; told him I will pay him as soon as I receive my terminal paycheck. I owe him a balance of $451. Sent out copies to David Lawrence (of *U.S. News & World Report*), James Burnham, Sidney Hook, Dr. Victor Sobey, two to Dr. Eva Reich, William Steig, A. S. Neil, J. Edgar Hoover, five to the Summerhill Society.

March 6, 1959: Headline in *Daily Argus:*

BOARD VOTES DISMISSAL OF SUSPENDED TEACHER

The "formalities" have been duly carried out!

The Great Silence now settles over the entire matter. No more phone calls or letters.

Received my terminal pay, and can now pay off my debts. We will stamp the dust of this town from our feet and go to Alaska.

FOOTNOTES TO HISTORY

March 9, 1959: from the *Daily Argus:*

CHILDREN BUT NOT PARENTS
DISLIKE "TREASURE ISLAND"

PHILADELPHIA (AP)—Robert Louis Stevenson's "Treasure Island" appears to have slipped a bit in the estimate of younger readers, but it still has a lot of partisans among the oldtimers who read it years ago.

An announcement by a committee of public school teachers that Stevenson's juvenile classic was to be dropped from the list of approved textbooks caused little concern among the kids, but their elders raised a flurry about the matter. . . .

March 10, 1959: from the *Daily Argus:*

"Outraged" Parents Told
To Identify Themselves

The Board of Education has a terse bit of advice for the "Outraged Americans" who in an anonymous letter complained recently about restrictions on students at Nichols School who wish to take academic course electives.

"Tell us who you are," said the school trustees at their monthly meeting.

Said Anthony J. Scarpino, board president, "If people are not willing to sign their names I don't think the board should waste its time with them."

So, Mr. Anthony J. Scarpino, president of the Mount Vernon Board of Education, doesn't like the taste of the very same medicine I received! I was *fired* for refusing to respond to anonymous complainants. I was never informed of precisely who was complaining about precisely *what*—just given verbal "charges" on the basis of nebulous "complainants." What cooked my goose is now choking Mr. Scarpino's gander.

We will go to the wilderness of Alaska. My students will never forget, and neither will I. I foresee the total disintegration of the educational process, rootless in the knowledge of Truth and Life. Fascism of the Left or the Right is coming. There is nothing more I can do here.

Part Five
The Emotional Plague Versus Genital Man

The following documents are published so that the Students of the Future might better understand the nature of the planetary Enemy of Mankind who seeks but one goal: *Ruthless and uncompromising control of the emotional and physical lives of all mankind.*

Whether Truth or Falsehood, Love or Hate will govern this planet will ultimately depend upon your ability to distinguish between the one or the other, and your willingness to support or oppose either.

The first document consists of extracts from *The Communist Manual of Instructions for Psychopolitical Warfare,* first brought to the attention of the U.S. Congress and the American people by Kenneth Goff, a former member of the American Communist Party. Now a strong anti-Communist, Mr. Goff wrote me in 1965 attesting to the authenticity of the *Manual for Psychopolitical Warfare,* and I reproduce his letter below:

Aug. 6, 1965

Jerome Eden
Staten Island, N.Y.

Dear Sir:

In the front cover of my book on PSYCHOPOLITICS, I have placed a statement concerning Eugene Debs' Labor School.

It can be verified that I attended this school in Vol. 9 of the Dies Committee Report, in which I gave testimony on Oct. 9th and 10th, 1939.

I have in my files a copy of the orientation manual, mimeographed form, which we used on Psychopolitics, and which I have quoted verbatim on Brain Washing. . . .

Sincerely yours for Christ and America,
/s/ Kenneth Goff

I urge you Students of the Future to view the following extracts with deadly *seriousness!* I warn you—as I warned you back in 1959 when I published *Suffer the Children*—that you must not confuse the "ideal" of Communism as a *goal*, with the *reality* of Red Fascism, the organized emotional plague of man. Milovan Djilas saw clearly through the subterfuge of "Communism" when he wrote:

> *Throughout history there have been no ideal ends which were attained with non-ideal, inhumane means, just as there has been no free society which was built by slaves. Nothing so well reveals the reality and greatness of ends as the methods used to attain them.°*

It was the Russian Commissar Lavrenti Beria, head of the Soviet Secret Police, who conceived of the tenets of Psychopolitical Warfare. Kenneth Goff identified *The Communist Manual of Instructions for Psychopolitical Warfare* as the manual used for training of Soviet agents in the United States at the Eugene Debs Labor School in Milwaukee, Wisconsin.

What follows now are verbatim extracts from this Manual:

BRAINWASHING

Chap. I—Psychopolitics is the art and science of asserting and maintaining dominion over the thoughts and loyalties of individuals, officers, bureaus, and masses, and the effecting of the conquest of enemy nations through 'MENTAL HEALING." (Note how every scientific advance, wherever possible, is used for *power-purposes* by the Fascist Pestilence. "Enemies of the State" are not necessarily "liquidated," but are rather jailed in *Insane Asylums!* JE)

Chap. II—The individual must be directed from without to accomplish his exercise, education, and work. . . . The tenets of rugged individualism, personal determinism, self-

---

°*The New Class*, New York, Frederick A. Praeger, Inc., 1957.

will, imagination, and personal creativeness are . . . anti-pathetic to the good of the Greater State. These willful and unaligned forces are no more than illnesses.

Chap. III— . . . one must . . . create and continue a semi-privation in the masses in order to command and utterly control the nation. . . . Communism (read "Organized Emotional Plague, JE) could best succeed if at the side of every rich or influential man there could be placed a psycho-political operator, an undoubted authority in the field of mental healing" who could then . . . upset the economic policies of the country and, when the time comes to do away forever with the rich or influential man . . . administer the proper drug or treatment to bring about his complete demise in an institution as a patient or dead as a suicide. . . .

The Capitalist does not know the definition of war. He thinks of war as an attack with force performed by soldiers and machines. . . . The Capitalist has never won a war in truth. The psychopolitician is having little trouble win-ning this one.

Chap. IV—Without pain there can be no desire to escape pain. Without the threat of punishment there can be no gain. . . . Without rigorous and forthright control, there can be no accomplished goals for the State. . . .

Chap. V—ANY MAN WHO CANNOT BE PER-SUADED INTO COMMUNIST RATIONALE IS, OF COURSE, TO BE REGARDED AS SOMEWHAT LESS THAN SANE, AND IT IS, THEREFORE, COMPLETELY JUSTIFIED TO USE THE TECHNIQUES OF INSANITY UPON THE NON-COMMUNIST. . . .

When the loyalty of an individual cannot be swerved . . . it is usually best . . . to see to it that he disposes of him-self by suicide or by bringing about his demise in such a way as to resemble suicide. . . . It is a firm principle of Psy-chopolitics that the person to be destroyed must be involved at first or second hand in the stigma of insanity. . . . (Reich is "crazy"; orgone energy doesn't exist! JE)

One of the first and foremost missions of the psycho-politician is to make an attack upon Communism and insanity synonymous. IT SHOULD BECOME THE DEFINITION OF INSANITY, OF THE PARANOID VARIETY, THAT "A PARANOID BELIEVES HE IS BEING ATTACKED BY COMMUNISTS."

Under the saccharine guise of assistance to them, rigorous child labor laws are the best means to deny the child any right in the society. By refusing to let him earn, by forcing him into unwanted dependence upon a grudging parent . . . the child can be driven in his teens into revolt. Delinquency will ensue. . . .

If we could effectively kill the national pride and patriotism of just one generation we will have won that country. . . .

The handling of youth cases by courts should be led . . . into "mental problems" until the entire nation thinks of "mental problems" instead of criminals. This places vacancies everywhere in the courts . . . which could then be filled with psychopolitical operators . . . and into their hands comes *the total control of the criminal, without whose help a revolution cannot ever be accomplished.* (Already in the mid-1960s and 1970s in the United States, we see the radicalization of youth and criminals well advanced. JE)

By stressing this authority . . . even the armed services will use "authorities on the mind" . . . and when this occurs the Armed Forces of the nation enter into our hands as solidly as if we commanded them ourselves.

Chap. VI—Any organization which has the spirit and courage to display inhumanity, savageness, brutality, and an uncompromising lack of humanity will be obeyed. Such use of force is itself, the essential ingredient of greatness . . .

. . . If you would have obedience you must make it clearly understood that you have no mercy. . . . Only when a person has been beaten, punished, and mercilessly hammered, can hypnotism upon him be guaranteed in its effectiveness. . . .

The subject of hypnotism is a subject of belief. . . . Despicable religions, such as Christianity, knew this. . . . The earliest Russian psychiatrists . . . understood thoroughly that hypnosis is induced by acute fear. . . .

. . . The psychiatrist is aptly suited to his role, for his brutalities are committed in the name of science and are inexplicably complex, and entirely out of view of the human understanding. As long as the psychopolitical operative or his dupes are the only authorities as to the difference between sanity and insanity, their word as to the therapeutic value of such treatment will be the final word.

It is to the interest of the psychopolitical operative that the possibility of curing the insane be outlawed and ruled out at all times. . . .

. . . The entire field of human behavior . . . can, at length, be broadened into abnormal behavior. Thus, anyone indulging in any eccentricity, particularly the eccentricity of combatting psychopolitics, could be silenced.

The entire subject of psychopolitical hypnosis . . . depends for its defense upon continuous protest from authoritative sources *that such things are not possible.* And should anyone unmask a psychopolitical operative, he should at once declare the whole thing a physical impossibility. . .

(The Student of the Future is urged to study again the chapter on "The Double-Squeeze Technique of the Emotional Plague," and carefully consider the Soviet warning that mind control *should not be used as a weapon of war* JE)

Chap. VII—Having no independent will of his own

Man (read "the victim," JE) is easily handled by stimulus-response mechanisms . . . an entire chain of commands . . . can be beaten, shocked, or terrorized into a mind, and will there lie dormant until called into view by some similarity . . . to the incident of punishment. . . . Exercise in sexual attack on patients should be practiced by the psychopolitical operative to demonstrate the inability of the patient under pain-drug hypnosis to recall the attack.

Chap. VIII—In order to be conquered, a nation must be degraded. . . . Continual and constant degradation of national leaders, national institutions, national practices, and national heroes must be systematically carried out. . . . The first thing to be degraded in any nation is the state of Man, himself. Nations which have high ethical tone are difficult to conquer. (The cesspool of pornography overwhelming America is a direct result of this dictum. JE)

Chap. IX—Psychopolitical operatives should at all times be alert to the opportunity to organize "for the betterment of the community" Mental Health Clubs or groups. By thus inviting the cooperation of the population as a whole in mental health programs, the terrors of mental aberration can be disseminated throughout the populace. Furthermore, each one of these mental health groups properly guided, can bring legislative pressure against the government to secure . . . government grants and facilities, thus bringing a government to finance its own downfall. . . .

It is not too much to hope that the influence of such groups could bring about a psychiatric ward in every hospital in the land, and psychiatrists in every company and regiment of the nation's army, and whole government institutions manned entirely by psychopolitical operatives, into which ailing (read "those opposed to Communism," JE) government officials could be placed. . . .

The psychopolitician may well find himself under attack

as an individual or a member of a group. . . . The best
defense is calling into question the sanity of the attacker.
The next best defense is authority. The next best defense is
a validation of psychiatric practices in terms of long and im-
pressive figures. The next best defense is the actual removal
of the attacker . . . but it is dangerous.

PSYCHOPOLITICS SHOULD AVOID MURDER AND
VIOLENCE, UNLESS IT IS DONE IN THE SAFETY OF
THE INSTITUTION. . . . (Reich "died" in a federal peni-
tentiary one week before he was to be released. JE)

Should any whisper, or pamphlet, against psychopolitical
activities be published, it should be laughed into scorn,
branded as an immediate hoax, *and its perpetrator or publisher should be, at the first opportunity, branded as insane.*

Chap. X—In the United States we have been able to
alter the works of William James and others, into a more
acceptable pattern, and to place the tenets of Karl Marx,
Pavlov, Lamarck, and the data of Dialectic Materialism
into the textbooks of psychology, to such a degree that
anyone thoroughly studying psychology becomes at once a
candidate to accept the reasonableness of Communism.

As every chair of Psychology in the United States is
occupied by persons in our connection, or who can be influ-
enced by persons in our connection, the consistent employ-
ment of such texts is guaranteed. . . .

Constant pressure in the legislature of the United States
can bring about legislation to the effect that every student
attending a high school or university must have classes in
psychology. (Classes in sexual promiscuity and pornography, under the guise of "sex education" are also rapidly
becoming mandatory. JE)

Chap. XII—Starting from a relatively low level of
violence, such as straight-jackets and other restraints, it is
relatively easy to encroach upon the public diffidence for
violence by adding more and more cruelty into the treat-

ment of the insane. . . . Gradually the public should be educated into electric shock, first by believing that it is very therapeutic, then by believing that it is quieting. . . . The more violent the treatment, the more hopeless insanity will seem to be. (One should also note here that any *effective* therapy, be it psychiatric orgone therapy, better nutrition, the use of natural foods, vitamins and minerals, or any other *natural* healing methods will be ridiculed or persecuted by the Red Fascist pestilence. JE)

The society should be worked up to the level where every recalcitrant young man can be brought into court and assigned to a psychopolitical operative, to be given electric shocks (or drugs, JE) and reduced into unimaginative docility for the remainder of his days. . . .

Chap. XIII—The psychopolitical dupe is a well-trained individual who serves in complete obedience the psychopolitical operative. . . . The promise of *unlimited sexual opportunities,* the promise of complete dominion over the bodies and minds of helpless patients, the promise of complete lawlessness without detection, can thus attract to "mental healing" many desirable recruits who will willingly fall in line with psychopolitical activities.

Chap. XIV—You must recruit every agency of the nation marked for slaughter into a foaming hatred of religious healing. . . . YOU MUST WORK UNTIL "RELIGION" IS SYNONYMOUS WITH INSANITY.

Chap. XV—Any movement to place clergymen in charge of institutions should be fought on the grounds of incompetence and insanity brought about by religion. . . .

A country's laws must be carefully made to avoid any rights of person to the insane. Any suggested laws or Constitutional Amendments which make the harming of the insane unlawful, should be fought to the extreme, on the grounds that only violent measures can succeed. If the law were to protect the insane, as it normally does not, the entire psychopolitical program would very possibly collapse.

. . . NO RECOVERY OF THE INSANE FROM AN INSTITUTION SHOULD BE POSSIBLE BY ANY PROCESS OF LAW. (Note well, Students of the Future: A murderer, a child-abuser-and-killer, may go free; but an Enemy of Communism must never go free. He must be "brainwashed," left to rot, or "liquidated." JE)

Any inquest into the "suicide" or sudden mental derangement of any political leader in a nation must be conducted only by psychopolitical operatives or their *dupes*. (Note well, liberals and leftist-sympathizers, how "highly regarded" you are. Following the immediate liquidation of anti-Red Fascists, you will be the next to "disappear"! JE)

Chap. XVI—The failure of Psychopolitics might well bring about the atomic bombing of the Motherland. (It might also bring about planetary *Peace!* But that is *not* the motivating drive of Red Fascism, which must constantly incite the chaos which is a prerequisite to its final global control. JE)

The spread of Communism (read "Fascism," JE) has never been by force of battle, but *by conquest of the mind*. In psychopolitics we have refined this conquest to the last degree.

A DANGEROUS EQUATION

In volume 1, number 1, of *FORE*, "A Journal for Orgonomic Education," which I published in January 1960 in Valdez, Alaska, I wrote the following article, entitled "A Dangerous Equation," in order to clarify the confusion over Communism as a political ideal and Red Fascism, the *reality* that governs millions today. The article follows.

"A DANGEROUS EQUATION"*

In June 1959, the Summerhill Society distributed a review of my book *Suffer the Children*. The review was written by A. S. Neill (Director of Summerhill). Although Neill holds a unique and well-deserved place as a pioneering functional educator, it is necessary to take issue with an attitude expressed in his review. It is an attitude which is far too widely held by the general public in the USA and abroad—an attitude which, in reality, is a dangerous equation that has resulted in past and present social consequences of the gravest kind.

Following are excerpts from Neill's review:

> Many books on children and education make most boring reading, so that when a book like this comes along it refreshes us a lot. Eden has some of Reich's drive and anger and fighting spirit. He is no shadow boxer; he hits with a straight left. He fights with indignation; he is really incensed about the way the world treats its children. To those unfamiliar with Reich's work much of this book may appear arresting, vivid, challenging; to others, to me for example, he gets at the root of matters and he is always on the side of the child. . . . *I think that, like Reich himself, he has made too much of Red Fascism and Communism as arch enemies of basic life. . . .*
>
> I fear that Reich and Eden and other American writers show symptoms of having lived in a hateful McCarthy era. . . . It is unlikely that they could escape from fear and from losing some perspective. . . . (Italics added. JE)

The heart of the issue here is Neill's equation of Red nd Black Fascism with "political parties," and not, as Dr. eich repeatedly stressed, the ORGANIZED EMOTIONAL LAGUE. (See Reich's *The Mass Psychology of Fascism*,

*Reprinted from *FORE*, Vol. 1, No. 1, January 1960, the Eden Press, ldez, Alaska.

People in Trouble, The Murder of Christ.) Furthermore, to state that "Reich himself has made too much of Red Fascism and Communism as arch enemies of basic life," bears witness to an ignorance of the Red Fascist conspiracy that resulted in the death of Dr. Reich and the burning and banning of his books in the USA. Such an ignorance in the general public is, to say the least, distressing. To find it expressed by someone with Neill's knowledge of Dr. Reich's long labor is astounding! In view of Neill's authoritative position, it is necessary to remember that his views concerning Red and Black Fascism are those primarily of an educator. Dr. Reich's evaluation of the Fascist pestilence is based upon personal and professional experience and clinical investigation in medicine, psychiatry, social psychiatry, bio-psychiatry and bio-energetics. No one who is at all familiar with the trial records and suppressed evidence of the case against orgonomy and Dr. Reich could say that "Reich made too much of Red Fascism." Let us not for one moment forget that Dr. Reich was killed by it!

In *Suffer the Children,* the very first sentence of the Introduction begins, "Under the term Fascism is subsumed all tyranny (be it in the home, the classroom, or the government), all acts and processes that utilize measures which are contrary to the fulfillment of basic human needs, and which limit or restrict man's inherent and inalienable right to express his Natural, God-given genital love—"

Throughout the book, I use Dr. Reich's equation of The Emotional Plague *equals* Red and Black Fascism. Again for instance, on page 134:

> After twenty centuries of "Progress" we still face the Scourge of Man, bigger, more powerful than ever, now fully mechanized and organized as Red and Black Fascism. It you value your life and the lives of your children, learn to read and understand the expressions of hate-enraged armored madmen whose only purpose is THE DESTRUCTION OF ALL LIVING LIFE, based upon their own HATRED OF THE LIVING.

In his "Writ of Certiorari" to the U.S. Supreme Court, Dr. Reich states:

> It is, most regrettably, unknown that Karl Marx was the first to dissolve a communist organization, the "Kommunisten Bund" in Germany in 1847. Already then a rampant Little Man philosophy of power drunkenness, combined with lack of will to learn, had appeared on the scene, foreshadowing, as it were, the mass murders of the Stalinite-Hitler type of one hundred years later. . . .
>
> Having been deeply immersed in misery over the ages, a period of written history of some 10 millennia, they want freedom, but they do not know what freedom really is like, how difficult, responsible, exacting at times to hold, to preserve and to develop. They [the people, JE] learned to *die* for freedom or liberties or abstract ideas. Now they die en masse in their own confusions. The *leaders of the confusion* are organized psychopathic individuals in government ("Higs", i.e., Hoodlums in Government) who abuse to their own pathological ends the confusion of the past and present in the human multitudes: FASCISM in all its colors in political parlance; Organized Emotional Plague in the parlance of Bio-Psychiatry. . . .

NEW LAWS NEEDED TO RESTRAIN PATHOLOGICAL POWER DRUNKENNESS*

BY WILHELM REICH, M.D., COUNSEL FOR THE LIFE ENERGY

FIRST: ON LAWFULNESS OF LAWS

All new laws proclaiming to govern human conduct in a growing and developing planetary society are designed to secure life, liberty and happiness for all. They must be *lawful* laws. They must not be unlawful laws. Laws must

---

*From Wilhelm Reich's "Petitioner's Reply Brief" to the U.S. Supreme Court, October Term, 1956, No. 688.

be based on facts, not on opinions; on truth, not on false-hood. Unlawful orders are automatically null and void.

SECOND: ON WELLSPRINGS OF SOCIAL EXISTENCE

Love, Work and Knowledge are the wellsprings of our existence. They are the wellsprings of our life, liberty and happiness with equal justice for all. They shall govern the future planetary social organization.

THIRD: ON LIFE-NECESSARY WORK

Life-necessary work and *naturally grown interhuman relationships* shall determine the lawfulness of laws, social responsibility and social guidance. Life-necessary work and natural interhuman relationships comprise *Natural Work Democracy*.

FOURTH: ON UNLAWFUL LAWS

Laws and orders which contradict, impede, destroy or otherwise endanger the development of self-determination and violate peaceful development, shall be null and void.

FIFTH: ON PROTECTION OF TRUTH

Social battles for truthful procedure are lawful battles. Procedures for elimination, evasion, eradication or falsification of factual truth are unlawful.

5-1. Juries, judges, magistrates and other judicial persons or bodies must render their verdicts fully informed on all pertinent facts involved in the case. Verdicts based on untruth, suppression or falsification of evidence are unlawful and intrinsically void.

5-2. Social administration must not interfere with the search for factual truth and basic new knowledge.

5-3. *Learning is the only authority on Knowledge of the Future.* There are no authorities in undisclosed realms of nature or New Knowledge. Learning and improving ability to find and correct one's mistakes are, among others, true characteristics of bona fide research.

5-4. Scientific tools and publications based on learning and search for new knowledge must never be controlled, censored or in any other way molested by any administrative agency of society. Such acts are unlawful, only perpetrated in dictatorships.

5-5. Bona fide scientists, i.e., men and women engaged in learning and searching for new knowledge, must not be ever dragged into courts of justice for their opinions or be harassed by commercial or political interests of the day.

5-6. The citizen has the constitutional right to ignore complaints against him *IF* he can prove to the satisfaction of the court that:

A. He has informed the court of his reasons for ignoring the complaint;

B. His reasons to ignore the complaint were weighty, based on proof of fraudulent presentations of fact, on motives to complain other than bona fide grievances, on a competitive conspiracy using illegal means, etc.;

C. The judge has been victimized, misled, or otherwise prejudiced;

D. Responding to the complaint would have meant inevitable undeserved disaster.

"A," in conjunction with either of "B," "C" or "D," constitutes sufficient reason lawfully not to appear in court as defendant.

5-7. *Disclosure of scientific information must not be forced* under any circumstances, by anyone or for whatever reasons.

5-8. *New knowledge requires new administrative laws.*

Laws applicable in one defined realm cannot be applied in a different realm of social or natural functioning.

5-9. *Judicial errors must be realized and corrected.* They must not be perpetuated to the detriment of justice. Perpetuation of judicial errors for whatever reason is unlawful.

5-10. *Judicial procedures which are shown to hamper truth and fact and run counter to the very meaning of due process of law,* which is to safeguard indivisible factual truth, *are to be revised or abolished.*

a) Judges acting in courts of justice are responsible for the safety of truth and fact from any interference by expediency, negligence, political or commercial interests. Judges are administrators of truth and justice, and nothing else.

b) *There is no excuse whatever for judicial error.* The innocent must not fall prey to faulty procedure. Judges are as law officers subjected to the *Boomerang Law* in case of gross neglect of justice. They shall suffer what they meted out unjustly.

c) Judges are to be appointed on the basis of their judicial expertness, not on any other, political, racial, commercial or similar grounds.

d) Judges may only interpret statutory laws. They may not legislate themselves under our Constitution.

e) Judges must not be beneficiaries or advocates of religious, commercial or political enterprises. Their only realm of functioning is jurisprudence and jurisdiction under the Constitution of the U.S.A., in pursuit of common law decency, truth, fact, above-board activity, absence of deceit, etc.

SIXTH: ON ENEMIES OF MANKIND

Individuals, legal persons, organizations and social groupings which advocate or operate on lines adverse to common natural laws or laws under the Constitution, or I to IV of the "New Law," shall be excluded from determining the course of society. They may *talk* against work democracy, but they may *not act* against the socially-organized rule of Love, Work and Knowledge. As *ENEMIES OF MANKIND,* they may not be elected to public office. Those lawfully declared to be Enemies of Mankind, if insisting on acts of fiendship against the self-rule of Love, Work and Knowledge, shall be subjected to the Seventh Law.

SEVENTH: ON BOOMERANG JUSTICE

Officers of the law, officials of a self-governing society and other highly placed responsible citizens (of the Planet Earth) shall be, if necessary, called before courts of justice to answer charges of *"treason to mankind."* If convicted upon *factual* evidence of treason, they shall be subjected to the *BOOMERANG LAW:* They shall suffer themselves whatever they may have planned against the planetary citizens who through safeguarding *Love, Work* and *Knowledge* as the natural foundations of a self-governing social system have secured true justice at the very source of social life.

EIGHTH: ON STRIKING OBSOLETE LAWS

In order to secure social rational progress and to prevent the development of irrational human adherence to untimely or hampering tradition, statutory laws which are no longer representing or reflecting living, actual reality shall be stricken from the statute books ("Statutory Rape").

NINTH: ON SAFETY OF NATURAL LOVE

Natural love functions leading up to and expressed in natural courting mating shall be considered *natural functions at the very basis of man's bioenergetic existence.* They shall be protected and secured by special laws. Human activities adverse to this basic natural function shall be prohibited by lawful procedures insofar as they tend to impede or destroy these natural love functions in infants, children, adolescents and grown-ups. Abuse of natural love functions for political, conspiratorial, commercial, pathological (unnatural) and similar purposes is in violation of this law.

TENTH: ON SUPERVISION OF UNLAWFULNESS OF LEGAL PROCEDURES

A new legislative body in Congress shall be established by way of amendment of the Constitution to constantly survey and supervise judiciary and law enforcement procedures. This committee shall be responsible to the people and their organizations of life-necessary work, not only for security of justice, truth and fact; it shall safeguard the constitutional laws which guarantee the development of society to ever more complete self-government of nations, organizations and responsible citizens.

BIBLIOGRAPHY

RECOMMENDED READING ON ORGONOMY

By Wilhelm Reich, M.D. Published by Farrar, Straus & Giroux, New York. Books may be ordered through any good bookstore:

Function of the Orgasm
The Cancer Biopathy
Selected Writings
Character Analysis
Ether, God and Devil/Cosmic Superimposition
Listen, Little Man!
The Mass Psychology of Fascism
The Sexual Revolution
The Murder of Christ
Reich Speaks of Freud
The Invasion of Compulsory Sex-Morality

Elsworth F. Baker. *Man in the Trap*. New York: Avon, 1974.
Jerome Eden. *Orgone Energy—The Answer to Atomic Suicide*. Hicksville, New York: Exposition Press, 1972.
Jerome Eden. *Planet in Trouble—The UFO Assault on Earth*. Hicksville, New York: Exposition Press, 1973.
Wilhelm Reich. *The Impulsive Character*, Translated by Barbara G. Koopman. New York: New American Library, 1974.

The Journal of Orgonomy. Orgonomic Publications, Inc., Box 565, Ansonia Station, New York, N.Y. 10023.

Ola Raknes. *Wilhelm Reich and Orgonomy.* New York: St. Martin's, 1970.

Peter Reich. *A Book of Dreams.* New York: Harper & Row, 1973.

Eden Bulletin (Based on Reich's UFO research): Box 34. Careywood, Idaho 83809.

Printed in Great Britain
by Amazon